P9-EMH-913

Why Do People Kiss the

Blarney Stone?

...AND 176 OTHER FASCINATING IRISH TRIVIA QUESTIONS

Ryan Hackney & Amy Hackney Blackwell

Avon, Massachusetts

Published by
Adams Media, a division of F+W Media, Inc.
57 Littlefield Street, Avon, MA 02322. U.S.A.
www.adamsmedia.com

ISBN 10: 1-4405-6005-6
ISBN 13: 978-1-4405-6005-7
eISBN 10: 1-4405-6006-4
eISBN 13: 978-1-4405-6006-4

Printed in the United States of America.

10   9   8   7   6   5   4   3   2   1

Contains portions of material adapted and abridged from *The Everything® Irish History and Heritage Book* by Ryan Hackney and Amy Hackney Blackwell, copyright © 2004, F+W Media, Inc., ISBN 10: 1-58062-980-6, ISBN 13: 978-1-58062-980-5; and *101 Things You Didn't Know about Irish History* by Ryan Hackney and Amy Hackney Blackwell, copyright © 2007, F+W Media, Inc., ISBN 10: 1-59869-323-9, ISBN 13: 978-1-59869-323-2.

Interior illustrations © 123rf.com.

This book is available at quantity discounts for bulk purchases.
For information, please call 1-800-289-0963.

CONTENTS

Part 4: Christianity on Celtic Shores 55

Part 5: The Rise of the Vikings 81

Part 6: Enter the British 95

Part 7: The Protestant Ascendancy and the Roman Catholic Church 109

Part 8: The Irish Potato Famine 127

Part 9: Independence and Irish Nationalism . 141

Part 14: Irish Literature........................ 221

Part 15: Geography and Climate...............231

Introduction

The island of Ireland transcends both its geographical and political boundaries. This transcendence has not occurred because of either a powerful military or economic presence. It has, in fact, occurred despite the notable lack of either. Instead, Ireland can be found on every continent through the memories, stories, and dreams of the immigrants, exiles, and friends who treasure Irish culture. But how much do you really know about the Emerald Isle?

Whether you don't know much about Ireland and want to learn more or you've read the *Tain* and touched the bullet holes in the General Post Office on O'Connell Street, you've come to the right place! In *Why Do People Kiss the Blarney Stone?* you'll find answers to questions like:

- ♣ What are fairy mounds?
- ♣ How can you catch a leprechaun?
- ♣ What was the Easter Rebellion?
- ♣ How do you pour the perfect pint?
- ♣ What was the Good Friday Agreement?
- ♣ How did *seanachaís* spin yarns?
- ♣ Did giants really build the Giant's Causeway?

And with all-encompassing topics ranging from mythology (Who was the Celtic Achilles?) to the Great Potato Famine (How did wearing pauper's uniforms save some Irish from starving?) to the gift of gab and storytelling (Why do Irish cats sleep inside?), you're sure to find everything you need to know about Ireland, her culture, and her history. You'll also find a primer of the Irish language at the back of the book that goes over basic Irish pronunciation, which will be helpful as you read all the Irish names and words throughout. So get ready to see if your Ireland IQ is as green as the fields of Athenry or as set in stone as the dolmens of the Burren. Enjoy!

PART 1

Early Ireland

Ireland is an island with an ancient and colorful past. People lived there for millennia before anyone started recording history, and they left their mark on the landscape— standing stones, odd-looking structures, great mounds of earth. The presence of so many prehistoric remains, many of which are pre-Celtic, ties Ireland's past to its present. What do you know about early Ireland?

WHY WOULD EARLY IRISH SETTLERS NEED SNOWSHOES?

Compared with the European mainland, Ireland hasn't been inhabited for very long. Africa, the Middle East, and central Europe have all housed humans for hundreds of thousands of years, and evidence suggests humans lived in England at least 250,000 years ago. But it was only about 9,000 years ago that anyone ventured to the Emerald Isle. Why was this? One word: ice.

Ireland was covered with ice for a very long time. It had few plants, and the only animals who lived there were creatures that preferred snow and ice, such as reindeer, woolly mammoths, and the spectacular Irish giant deer. The temperature fluctuated, but mostly just in variations on the same theme of cold.

IRISH BLESSING

Health and a long life to you.
Land without rent to you.
A child every year to you.
And if you can't go to heaven,
May you at least die in Ireland.

About 13,000 years ago, the ice finally started to recede, and Ireland warmed up. This was bad for some of the larger mammals, which became extinct, but it was good for smaller creatures and plants. No one knows for sure how Ireland's wildlife got there; maybe the animals floated across the Irish Sea, or maybe a temporary bridge of land once existed between Ireland and England. In any case, by about 5000 B.C.E. Ireland was covered with forests and full of wild beasts.

WHAT'S THE IMPORTANCE OF IRELAND'S STONE TOOLS?

Ireland's early settlers did not leave behind much information about themselves. Mostly, archaeologists have found stone tools—things like axes, knives, and scrapers. People used these tools to chop plants or skin animals. Ireland is full of these stone tools, and amateur collectors have picked up many of them.

Flint is one of the best stones for toolmaking, and the best flint in Ireland is found in the northeastern corner. And that's where most of Ireland's stone tools have been found—in Antrim, Down, and the Strangford Lough area. One of the best Mesolithic sites is Mount Sandel in County Derry, where archaeologists have found the remains of several little dome-shaped huts, built there between 7010 and 6490 B.C.E. Here, people lived, huddled around their fires, eating nuts, berries, pigs, birds, and fish.

The Mesolithic Period, also known as the Middle Stone Age, lasted for several thousand years. Stone technology did not change much during this time. People lived a fairly migratory existence, moving around in pursuit of plants and animals. Around 4000 B.C.E., things changed. People began to grow food and make pottery. They cleared forests for their fields and built more permanent settlements. Archaeologists call this new period the Neolithic Period, or New Stone Age.

It's possible that the Mesolithic Irish developed this new technology on their own, but it's more likely that these changes came over the ocean with new immigrants. The newcomers either conquered the people already living there, or, more likely, they just assimilated them, intermarrying and sharing techniques for making tools and growing crops. This assimilation worked in both directions. It brought new things while keeping the old, and this layering was vital to Irish culture later.

Neolithic people built their houses out of wood. These houses have mostly decayed, but their stone foundations are still visible. Archaeologists have also found lots of new tools for grinding wheat and a huge number of polished stone axes made from a stone called porcellanite.

WHAT ARE FAIRY MOUNDS?

Stone Age people built a lot of tombs or tomblike structures out of gigantic rocks covered with mounds of earth. This building technique makes the tombs look like big, grassy mushrooms from the outside. These ancient tombs continue to intrigue people today; there are so many of them all over the landscape, they're hard to miss.

The megalithic tombs were probably constructed shortly before the arrival of the Celts, who called them "fairy mounds" and believed that the spirits of ancient people—bold heroes and brave maidens—lived there. The Celtic creator gods, the Tuatha Dé Danann, were known to be fabulously good at building things, and perhaps it was they who constructed the tombs dotting the countryside. Eventually, the spirits inhabiting the fairy mounds transformed into the little people of later

Irish legends—leprechauns, fairies, and brownies—whose spirits are said to haunt the land.

HOW DID THE EARLY IRISH BURY THEIR DEAD?

A variety of different tombs—or fairy mounds—where the early settlers buried and honored their dead can be found throughout Ireland. These tombs include:

* **Passage Tombs:** Many of the megalithic tombs are called passage tombs because they contain passages leading to burial chambers underneath the mounds. The walls of the passage and chamber are made of rock that is often elaborately carved.

* **Court Tombs:** Court tombs, or *cairns*, have an open, roofless courtyard in front leading into two, three, or four chambers at back. Archaeologists have found human remains in them but think that they might originally have been built as temples. They tend to be evenly distributed about 3 miles apart instead of clustered like graves. Generally structures that are spaced like that are places of worship, but there's no way to tell for sure how people used them.

* **Wedge Tombs:** Wedge tombs occur primarily in the northern part of Ireland. These tombs have stone walls and roofs; the roof gets lower and the passage narrower as you go into the tomb, hence the name "wedge." Most of them face west or southwest, toward the setting sun. Wedge tombs are numerous; there are

about 500 of them all over the northern part of the country, although some can be found on Ireland's eastern coastline. The ones that have been excavated contain human remains, and some contain pottery, which suggests they were made toward the end of the Neolithic period.

* **Portal Tombs:** Portal tombs, also called dolmens, consist of several large upright stones topped by a giant capstone. Putting these rocks in place must have been a stupendous effort—some capstones weigh as much as 100 tons. These dolmens were originally surrounded by mounds of earth, and people were buried inside them. A giant dolmen at Poulnabrone, County Clare, had more than twenty people buried in it over a 600-year period; this might mean that only royalty was buried there. Dolmens exist all over Ireland, as well as in Wales and Cornwall. The Kilclooney More dolmen in County Donegal is particularly impressive—its capstone is almost 14 feet long.

THE HAG'S BED

Labbacallee ("Hag's Bed"), in County Cork, is an excellent example of a wedge tomb. It got its strange name because, when it was first opened, it contained the skeleton of a headless woman.

WHY DID GRAVE ROBBERS LOOT BOYNE PALACE?

Some of the most spectacular archaeological sites from the Neolithic period are in the Boyne Valley in County Meath. These sites are called *Brú na Bóinne*, which means "Boyne Palace." They consist of large stone tombs built around 3200 B.C.E., several centuries before the great pyramids of Egypt. The three main components of this site are New-grange, Knowth, and Dowth, which people have known about for centuries. The Vikings plundered them; the Victorians hunted treasures there and carved their initials on the walls. The sites gradually deterio-rated and were even quarried at one time. The Republic of Ireland has become very interested in its history, however, and consequently, the tombs have been extensively restored.

The tombs at Newgrange are built inside a huge, grassy mound of earth. The stones at the entrance and some of the stones holding the tomb together are elaborately carved with spirals. These stones are not local; some of them came from Wicklow, 50 miles away, and others from Northern Ireland.

Rings of giant stones might have surrounded such tombs, though only twelve of these now remain. It sounds a little like Stonehenge, something to which the tomb has been compared.

Inside the mound is a long passageway leading to a subterranean burial chamber. Inside this chamber are three recesses for holding remains. The front door of Newgrange is a solar observatory extraor-dinaire. When the tomb was first excavated by experts, archaeologists found the remains of at least three cremated bodies and some human bones. Offerings of jewelry were probably there at one time as well, but grave robbers stole these long ago.

No one knows exactly why these mounds were built. They might have been burial places for kings; ancient legends certainly suggest that as a possibility. Or they might have served as calendars. Many megalithic sites are constructed to catch the sun at particular times of the year, and they are astonishingly accurate.

Newgrange is the best-known example of this. Every year during the winter solstice (December 19–23), the rising sun shines through a slit over the entrance and lights up the burial chamber for seventeen minutes. At the time the tomb was built, the sunlight would have shone directly on a spiral design carved into the wall.

WHY WERE BRONZE AND GOLD LIFE-CHANGING ON THE EMERALD ISLE?

Around 2400 B.C.E., people started making tools out of metal instead of stone. These metalworkers might have been a new wave of immigrants who brought their craft with them, or they might have been folks already in Ireland. Whoever they were, their metal tools were much better than stone ones.

This period is called the Bronze Age because most of these tools were made of bronze, an alloy of copper and tin mixed together. Ireland has tons of copper, and archaeologists have found traces of many copper mines. Tin is harder to get; people might have imported it from England or possibly from Brittany in France.

Smiths shaped bronze into all kinds of objects, including axes, spearheads, and jewelry. They decorated some of these with triangles and zigzags, which give the impression that these objects might have been more for show than for use.

Ireland also had a fair amount of gold hidden in its hills, and Bronze Age smiths used it to make some spectacular jewelry—thick bracelets and necklaces called torques, fancy hairpins, and half-moon-shaped trinkets that they probably hung around their necks. They also made discs of thin sheets of gold with hammered decorations; these are called sun discs, and people might have worn them as jewelry, too. Examples of these adornments can be seen at the National Museum of Ireland in Dublin.

WHAT ROLE DID BRITAIN PLAY IN CREATING A CELTIC IRELAND?

Around 800 B.C.E. the Bronze Age in Ireland ended and iron reigned supreme. This must have been the result of increased contact with Britain, which had closer contact with the rest of Europe, where iron was all the rage.

Early iron wasn't superior to bronze—in the days before steel was invented, iron was ugly and of poor quality. But iron ore was readily available almost everywhere, and supplies of tin, necessary for making bronze, were not. And so blacksmiths stuck with it and gradually got better at working iron.

The iron-using people also had horses. Archaeologists have found many bits for bridles and other tidbits of equestrian gear. They have also unearthed miles and miles of wooden tracks beneath the bogs, paths made of giant oak planks laid side by side; these would have made transporting goods by horse and cart much easier than dragging them through Ireland's soft soil.

The advent of iron is often associated with the arrival of the people called the Celts. By 300 B.C.E., the Celtic artistic style was thoroughly established in the northern part of Ireland. The Celts spread their culture and language throughout Ireland over the next several centuries, mixing their beliefs with Christianity and resisting foreign assailants as long as they could.

PART 2

The Rise of
Celts and Kings

Celtic culture is everywhere in Ireland, from the stone crosses in the countryside to patterns knit into wool sweaters. Modern Irish people still look back to their pre-English ancestors to get a feel for what their country should be today. The influence of the Celts is remarkable, considering how little is actually known about them. What do you know about these elusive Celts and kings of early Ireland?

WHO WERE THE CELTS?

It's hard to say anything conclusive about the Celts, because they didn't record their history themselves. They couldn't write and most everything we know about them today comes from either archaeological evidence or the accounts of Roman visitors that were transcribed by medieval Christians. This means that all of our written records about the Celts were filtered through two sets of biases: the Romans, who looked on the Celts as an alien culture that needed to be conquered, and the Christians, who thought the Celts were pagans who hadn't accepted the truth of Christ. And modern observers have all kinds of opinions that color their views.

you say *keltics,* I say *seltiks*

The word "Celt" is properly pronounced *kelt,* with a hard initial consonant. The name of the NBA team in Boston, however, is pronounced *seltiks.* If you encounter Celtics fans, don't try to correct their pronunciation.

According to classical writers, most of the people who lived in northwestern and central Europe were Celts—*keltoi* in Greek. Ancient writers knew of Celtic people in Spain, France, Germany, Switzerland, and modern Austria. Celts were hard to miss, because they were violent; various Celtic peoples started attacking Greek and Roman settlements around 400 B.C.E. and kept attacking so long as there was loot to be had.

Historians have long imagined ancient history as a series of peoples taking over land from one another. When they envisioned the Celts, they saw warriors who came marauding over the countryside, laying waste and taking over local wealth. Although there is some truth to this picture, it seems that cultural spread was actually a much gentler process most of the time. Celtic culture moved over the Continent and into the British Isles until, by the fourth century B.C.E., most of the people in northwestern Europe and Britain were members of this cultural group.

The people who became known as the Irish were probably a mix of indigenous peoples—remember the folks who built those mounds and tombs?—and immigrants who brought new languages and technology with them. The newcomers entered Irish society by marrying the natives, although there was probably some violence as well. Irish legend gives the impression that a bunch of warriors arrived several centuries before Christ and established chiefdoms for themselves all over the country. The Celtic languages became predominant either through military domination or because they were more prestigious for other reasons. However it happened, by the time the Romans arrived, the Irish people were speaking Celtic languages.

HOW MANY PROVINCES DOES IRELAND HAVE?

Back in the day, Ireland was divided into five areas:

1. Leinster—the southeast
2. Meath—the middle

3. Connacht—the west
4. Ulster—the north
5. Munster—the southwest

Later on, Meath was incorporated into Ulster and Leinster, which is why modern Ireland only has four provinces. Each of these provinces was divided into 100 or so smaller sections called *tuatha*, or tribes, each governed by its own chieftain, called a *rí*. People were divided into clans, and several clans made up a tribe. Ordinary people swore allegiance to their local king. Sometimes one man would rise above all the others and become high king of all Ireland.

PRESERVING THE ORAL TRADITION

People studying Ireland actually have an advantage over those scrutinizing Celts from other lands, because a number of ancient Irish stories and other writings survive. The Celts didn't write these things down themselves; they transmitted their culture orally. But centuries later, medieval monks, in their zeal to preserve stories of the oral tradition in written form, wrote down a bunch of ancient Celtic legends and books of laws, and these offer the modern reader a unique glimpse into ancient Irish life. This life seems to have included heroes, feasts, cattle raids, and love affairs.

HOW COULD THE *WARP-SPASM* GIVE YOU AN EDGE IN BATTLE?

The Irish were obsessed with war, weapons, and heroics. If their poetry is any indication, they spent most of their time at war with one another, stealing cattle, and feasting on pork.

The Celts scared the Romans and other "civilized" contemporary observers. When they went into battle, the Celts stripped naked and dashed at their enemies, wearing only sandals and their fancy necklaces. They howled as if possessed by demons, their shrieks accompanied by loud bagpipes. Some warriors became so overcome by battle-frenzy that their very appearances changed. They called this transformation the *warp-spasm*. The *Táin Bó Cuailnge* (see Part 3) has an excellent description of the hero Cuchulain (or Cú Chulainn) undergoing this phenomenon, during which most of his body turned itself inside out and fire and blood shot out of his head, after which he killed hundreds of enemy warriors and walked away unscathed.

Cattle and metal treasure were the main forms of wealth in ancient Ireland—metal because it was rare, and cattle because they were useful. Cattle provided milk to drink and to make into cheese, and hide and meat after they died. If a king demanded tribute from his subjects, it was usually in the form of cattle—in fact, a wealthy farmer was called a *bóiare*, or "lord of cows." Celtic chieftains spent quite a bit of their energy stealing cattle from one another. They even had a special word for this activity, *táin*. (Cattle raiding wasn't just something the ancient Irish did; modern Irish people were stealing one another's cattle well into the twentieth century.) Anyone whose cattle got stolen had to try to retrieve them, which occasioned many heroic expeditions and battles.

WHY IS TARA THE SEAT OF KINGS?

Tara, a hill in County Meath, was the seat of ancient Irish kings. It was considered the center of Ireland. People buried their ancestors in mounds surrounding it and periodically gathered there for festivals and rituals. Kings and their armies gathered there before marching to war.

Tara was special because it was the home of the *Lia Fáil*, or "Stone of Destiny," which was used to identify rightful kings—it shrieked if the feet of the rightful king rested on it.

WHY ARE THERE SO MANY FORTS IN IRELAND?

Ireland has tons of forts scattered all over the countryside, many of them built during the Bronze or Iron Ages and used for many centuries thereafter. The number and ingenuity of these forts suggest that the ancient Irish considered defense a high priority, though some experts think they were more likely built to impress. The most common form is the ring fort. These forts were built on top of circular mounds of earth with a wooden fence running around the circumference of the mound at the top and a moat surrounding the bottom.

Some forts were built entirely of stone or on the edges of cliffs, which provided a natural barrier to attack. Others, called *crannogs*, were built on artificial islands in the middle of lakes or bogs. They were used as late as the seventeenth century.

WHAT WERE THE BREHON LAWS?

Today, the best picture we have of ancient Irish social organization comes from the Brehon laws, which were written down in the seventh and eighth centuries C.E. These laws described a very structured society with several classes of people and clearly defined punishments for infractions.

For many years, historians believed that the Brehon laws came from the pre-Christian pagan past—possibly from the druids—and that they summarized centuries of laws and beliefs transmitted orally long before they were written. More recent scholars suggest that the Brehon laws were written by later Christians, who combined ancient Irish practices with foreign information and the Bible to create laws for the Irish people. Whether druid or Christian, the group of judges, lawyers, and professional poets who created these laws were called *breitheamh*, or brehons.

Brehon laws applied to civil, criminal, and military matters. They delineated five major classes of people and their rights and duties. All relationships, such as those between landlords and tenants, parents and children, and masters and servants, were carefully regulated.

Professionals were required to charge only the fees set by law, and they were ranked according to the status of their profession.

There were five classes of Irish people. At the top were the nobles, who belonged to the dominant families and owned property. Below them were ordinary freemen, who rented land and farmed it, and then base clients who had fewer rights. The lords gave their clients cattle, and in return received rents and other services. At the bottom were slaves. The fifth class of people was the group of learned men, including doctors, judges, poets, and craftsmen. Members of this group enjoyed special privileges and could move most freely outside their own clans.

SISTER WIVES

Brehon law also regulated marriage. A husband could take a second wife or, in the event of death or divorce, a subsequent wife, but the first wife had higher status than the second. The first wife received the second wife's bride price for her own and was allowed to do anything she wanted to the second wife (short of killing her) during the new wife's first three nights at home.

Brehon law generally did not punish wrongdoers, but a person who injured another was required to compensate his victim for the loss or to have the person nursed back to health at his expense. People could kill outlaws who had committed serious crimes, but kings could ransom these outlaws and get them freed of obligation—if, for example, a king's ally had committed some atrocious crime and another noble wanted to kill him, the king could ransom the ally and get him off the hook.

DID THE DRUIDS
PRACTICE MAGIC?

The druids were an ancient caste of learned men (and perhaps some learned women too, although there aren't any records that indicate this). What they learned and what they did has long been a matter of much discussion and debate. Herodotus claimed they were descended from Noah, originated in the western Danube region, and espoused Pythagorean philosophy. Pliny and Tacitus noted their fondness for the oak tree and their refusal to worship the gods under roofs. Julius Caesar described their schools, where they memorized vast amounts of information, and their sacrificial practices, which involved placing humans or animals in wicker cages and burning them alive. In Irish legends, druids can predict the future by interpreting the actions of birds; they use this information to advise their leaders when to march into battle. They wear white robes and sport long beards.

The Romans distrusted the druids and did their best to put them down. In 61 c.e. the Roman Suetonius rounded up a number of druids and killed them, and that ended druidism in Roman territory (which didn't include Ireland). But the druids were too fascinating for people to forget them; many still think of the megalithic dolmens (see Part 1) as druid altars, where the ancient priest-magicians sacrificed their victims.

One of the most famous is the druid Cathbad in the *Táin Bó Cuailnge*. In some versions of the story, he was the father of King Conchobar of Ulster (or Conor mac Nessa). Cathbad ran a school of druidry with eight students. After the hero Cuchulain accidentally killed his own son in battle, the soldiers of Ulster (on Cuchulain's side) feared he might kill them in his frenzied grief. Cathbad saved the army by casting a spell on Cuchulain to make him think the waves in the ocean were warriors, so he would fight them and expend his anger there.

WHY WERE CELTIC CRAFTSMEN SO HIGHLY REGARDED?

Celts held their craftsmen in high regard. Craftsmen belonged to a special privileged class of learned men, and the ordinary rules of serfdom and allegiance to a lord did not apply to them. They traveled from patron to patron plying their trades, and their status protected them from assault.

These Celtic craftsmen produced some spectacularly beautiful art. Much of their best work was done in gold, iron, and bronze. They used the lost-wax casting technique—molding an object out of wax, surrounding it with clay, baking the whole thing so the clay hardened and the wax ran out, and then pouring molten metal into the clay mold to form the object. They also formed objects out of sheets of metal, hammered thin and then cut and formed into the desired shape.

Celtic metalwork is intricately decorated and highly prized. The Celtic aristocrats liked to have nice things on hand to give as gifts to honored guests, which brought great honor to the giver, and they especially liked finely wrought metal. Celtic men and women wore heavy necklaces of twisted gold, called *torques*. These became status symbols, and the gods were also represented as wearing them.

Celtic burial sites are full of decorative pins called *fibulae*, which are similar in design to the modern safety pin. Archaeologists have also discovered mirrors, combs, and a beautiful little model boat with oars. Many of these artifacts are elaborately decorated with the distinctive spirals and interweaving designs for which the Celts are famous.

HOW DID POETS KEEP CELTIC CULTURE ALIVE?

Poets, like great craftsmen, were honored members of society, welcome in any noble home. They preserved the history of the clan and of Ireland, including the lore of the gods and the genealogy of the rulers. The ancient myths and legends were preserved by countless generations of poets, who memorized them and recited them to their listeners.

IRISH PROVERB

An Irishman is never drunk as long as he can hold on to one blade of grass and not fall off the face of the Earth.

Poets came in several grades; a poet of the highest status was equal to any chieftain. Training to become a poet took years and involved memorizing thousands of lines of verse. Poets were also reputed to know something about magic and prophecy. A patron expected a poet to sing his praises, but he had to be careful; poets demanded large rewards, and an unsatisfied poet could create burning satire that could ruin a chieftain's reputation.

DID THE ROMANS EVER CONQUER IRELAND?

The Romans never saw a land they didn't want to conquer, but they never conquered Ireland. Julius Caesar initiated contact with Britain in 55 B.C.E., and for over a century the Romans planned to conquer the whole island. Though some Britons became Romanized, many locals didn't appreciate being colonized and fought their conquerors tooth and nail. The Romans couldn't keep enough troops on the island to hold them at bay. They had other frontiers to guard, after all. By 122 C.E., Hadrian had decided it would be wise to wall off Scotland to keep the barbarians separate from Romanized territory. During the next two centuries, Rome gradually lost control over Britain.

The Romans knew Ireland existed; Ireland's Latin name is *Hibernia*, which might mean "Land of Winter." (Another theory holds that it comes from Iberia, or Spain.) Julius Caesar mentioned Ireland in his *Commentaries*, but only noted that it was less than half the size of Britain. The Greek geographer Strabo claimed Ireland was on the edge of the habitable Earth and that the inhabitants of the island were complete savages living a miserable existence due to the cold climate. The Roman Tacitus, writing around 100 C.E., thought Ireland was very much like Britain. In the late first century C.E., Agricola, a Roman governor of Britain, considered conquering Ireland and even did reconnaissance; he decided that the Romans could take the island with just one legion of soldiers, but it probably wouldn't be worth the effort.

The Romans never tried to conquer Ireland. The distance from Rome was too great and the potential payoff too uncertain, and they already had their hands full with Britain. And so the Irish remained Celtic.

PART 3

Celtic Mythology

Many Celtic myths and legends tell the stories of gods and goddesses and of ancient heroes—just like ancient Greek myths, but with a uniquely Celtic spin on things. These stories explain the origin of the Irish people, the relationship they had with their deities, and why certain people and places were more important than others. The Celts believed in many different gods and goddesses—gods of love, writing, light, death, and, of course, war—and that these deities had relationships with one another as well as with humans. How much do you know about Celtic mythology?

WHO WERE THE CELTIC GODS?

The Celts had a number of gods; here are a few of them:

- **The Daghdha**, or "Good God," was the chief god of the Irish pantheon. He carried a club that could both kill and bring people back to life. He also had a giant magic cauldron that was always full of food.
- **Donn** was the god of the dead. The druids claimed that all people were descended from him.
- **Oenghus** was the son of the Daghdha. He was a handsome young man and functioned something like a god of love.
- **Oghma** invented the ogham alphabet, a system of writing and divination used by druids.
- **Lug** was the sun god, god of genius and light. He was the hero Cuchulain's father. Julius Caesar thought that Lug was the most important Celtic god.
- **Nuadhu Airgedlámh** is an ancestor god-king. He lost an arm in battle and replaced it with one made of silver.
- **Dian Cécht** was the "Divine Physician." Mortally wounded people could be cast into a well and he would sing over it, after which they came out again healed.
- **Boibhniu** was the leader of three craftsman gods. He was also the host of the Otherworld Feast, at which he served a drink that made people immortal.
- **Manannán** was a sea god. He oversaw the journey across the sea to the otherworld.

These were not the only Celtic gods. Many others existed, though not all their names have been recorded. There are still strange statues in Ireland that depict fearful beings, many with two or three faces; who they were or what they did, no one knows.

Who were the Celtic goddesses?

The Celtic pantheon included a number of female deities. Many of them traveled in groups of three, such as the Macha-Mórrígan-Babd trio of war/fertility goddesses.

* **Anu**, or **Danu**, was the mother goddess and mother of the gods. She was connected with fertility and nurture.
* **Brigid** was the daughter of the Daghdha. She was a goddess of fertility and the patron of poets. She had two sisters, also named Brigid, who were associated with craftsmanship and healing; the three of them were often treated as one entity. Brigid's symbol was fire, and a fire was kept alight for her in County Kildare from pre-Christian times until 1151. She later transformed into the Christian St. Bride, or St. Brigid.
* A trio of sisters—**Macha (MA-ha), Mórrígan, and Babd (bahv)**—were known as the **Mórrígna**. They were war and fertility goddesses; they played an important part in the war between the Tuatha Dé Danaan and the Fomorians.

- **Mórrígan** embodied war fury. A number of sites in Ireland bear her name.
- **Babd** was both sinister and sexual; she sometimes appeared as a crow, sometimes as a hag, and sometimes as a beautiful young woman. She urged the hero Cuchulain to go fight his last battle, which led to his death.
- **Scáthach** was the "Shadowy One." She taught the young Cuchulain all his magic.
- **Boann** was a water goddess who embodied the spirit of the Boyne River. She and the Daghdha had a child together—Oenghus, who functioned something like the god of love.

home of the gods

The world of Celtic gods and spirits was known as the otherworld, Mag Mell ("Plain of Honey"), Tír Tairngire ("Land of Promise"), and Tír na nÓg ("Land of Perpetual Youth"). It was a place of simple and sensuous pleasures. Everyone living there could eat as much as they wanted, and many heroes found loving women there. The cauldron of the Daghdha—a cauldron that was always full of food—was there. Heroes would occasionally make special trips to the otherworld; these voyages were called *imrama* (or *immrama*). A famous legend called the *Imram Bran Maic Febail* is the story of the Irish king Bran's journey to the otherworld (in other versions, the journey is to the Land of Women).

HOW WERE THE GODS AND GODDESSES CELEBRATED?

The Celts divided the year into two halves, the bright, warm half known as *samh*, or summer, and the dark, cold half called *gamh*, or winter. They punctuated the year with four festivals marking the different seasons:

- ♣ **Imbolc (IM-bulk)** took place on February 1. It was the feast of the goddess Brigid, and associated with the birth of lambs and the lactation of ewes.
- ♣ **Beltane (BAL-thu-na)** was celebrated on May 1. People lit bonfires, danced around maypoles, and made merry. This feast marked the start of summer.
- ♣ **Lughnasa (LOO-na-sa)** was a harvest festival held in late summer in honor of the god Lug. Festivities included games, drinking, dancing, matchmaking, and racing horses while naked.
- ♣ **Samhain (SOW-in)** corresponds to modern Halloween and marked the end of summer. This is the day that tombs opened and ghosts walked about with gods and goddesses.

These festivals fall halfway between the solar equinoxes and solstices, all of which were easy to identify using the solar devices incorporated into various megalithic mounds. The Celts were masterful astronomers, given that they didn't have telescopes. They knew about the planets Mercury, Venus, Mars, Jupiter, and Saturn, and their year lasted 365 days.

WHAT IS THE MYTHOLOGICAL CYCLE?

According to legend, the island of Ireland was invaded six different times in its prehistory. The story of these invasions is told in a body of myth called the Mythological Cycle (a title that came about in the nineteenth and twentieth centuries), much of which was recorded in the twelfth century in the *Book of Invasions*. The ultimate consequence of all these invasions was a final battle between two groups of supernatural people, the Tuatha Dé Danaan and the Fomorians, and the establishment of civilization and social order.

WHY DID NOAH'S DESCENDANTS INVADE IRELAND?

The first invasion was led by one of the granddaughters of Noah (the biblical Noah who built the Ark), but her timing was bad; all of her people drowned in the great flood. Three hundred years later, another descendant of Noah, Parthalón, settled Ireland, building houses and clearing fields for farming. Parthalón's sworn enemies were the Fomorians, one-armed, one-legged monsters descended from Noah's cursed son, Ham.

Parthalón and his people all died of plague. Thirty years later, the third invasion arrived, led by a man named Nemhedh. They attacked the Fomorians, but most of them died in the effort. A few survivors fled to Greece, where they became slaves; they were called the Fir Bolg.

The Fir Bolg came back to Ireland, which they divided into the five provinces of the Celts. They established a kingship and ruled the land for thirty-seven years. Their last king, Eochaidh mac Eirc, was a perfect, just ruler. During his reign no rain fell, only dew; there was no year without a harvest; and nobody told any falsehoods. The Fir Bolg had a nice arrangement, but it was too good to last. Yet another group of people decided to invade Ireland: the Tuatha Dé Danaan.

WHO WERE THE TUATHA DÉ DANAAN?

The Tuatha Dé Danaan were the people of the mother goddess Anu. According to Irish legend, they arrived around 350 B.C.E. They came from four cities in ancient Greece, which is where they learned about prophecy and magic, the secrets of the druids. They brought with them four treasures:

- **The cauldron of the Daghdha:** This vessel was always full of food.
- **The spear of Lug:** This weapon ensured victory to its holder.
- **The sword of Nuadhu Airgedlámh:** No enemy could escape from it once it was drawn from its sheath.
- **The Lia Fáil:** Known as the "Stone of Destiny," it shrieked when the feet of a lawful king rested on it; this ended up on Tara Hill, seat of Irish kings.

The Tuatha Dé Danaan were skilled in magic and fighting. Their leader, Nuadhu Airgedlámh, brought them into battle. But a Fir Bolg warrior named Sreng cut his arm off at the shoulder. Sreng made peace with the Tuatha Dé Danaan and agreed to leave them all of Ireland except for Connacht (or Connaught), where he led his own people.

Poor Nuadhu Airgedlámh couldn't be king anymore, because no one with a physical defect (such as a missing arm) could be king. A man named Bres was elected to be king instead. Bres was the son of the Fomorian king Delbáeth; he had been adopted and raised by the Tuatha Dé Danaan, and they obviously thought they could trust him. But they were mistaken.

NOT-SO-SUPERNATURAL

Some scholars think that, in the original myths, the Tuatha Dé Danaan were divine, not the supernatural beings they appear to be. According to this theory, medieval monks who recorded the stories demoted the Tuatha Dé Danaan to their current stature, not wanting to suggest that other gods could rival the Christian one.

Bres, the Fomorian, ruled the Tuatha Dé Danaan for seven years, a terrible time for the Tuatha Dé Danaan. The Fomorians demanded a tribute of cattle, and the gods were reduced to menial labor; even the Daghdha himself was forced to dig ditches and build a fortress for Bres.

Meanwhile, the Tuatha Dé Danaan were planning their recovery. Dian Cécht, the "Divine Physician," made a new arm for Nuadhu out of silver, which would allow him to be king again. After a poet named Cairbre mac Étain (son of Étain) sang a verse mocking Bres, he gave up the kingship and went off to gather an army of his Fomorians. Nuadhu was reinstated as king; he and the Daghdha and Lug got together to decide how to get back at the Fomorians. (Lug had recently appeared at the court, and he had impressed everyone so much with his skill in all arts, creative and warlike, that they let him be one of their leaders.)

The Daghdha went to see Mórrígan at the festival of Samhain. She was standing astride the River Unius washing herself. They made love standing over the water, which gave that spot the name "Bed of the Couple." She told the Daghdha that the Fomorians were coming to attack the Tuatha Dé Danaan and that he should bring his soldiers to her. She killed the son of the Fomorian king and gave two handfuls of the blood to the Tuatha Dé Danaan before they went into battle. She and her sisters Babd and Macha went to the Mound of the Hostages at Tara and made the sky rain blood down onto the battle.

Lug led the Tuatha Dé Danaan in the second battle of Magh Tuiredh. The Mórrígan entered the fray, cheering on the Tuatha Dé Danaan and pursuing any Fomorians who tried to run away. Blood ran freely over the white-skinned warriors and the River Unius was clogged with corpses. Lug and his armies finally defeated the Fomorians and drove them to the sea.

After the fighting was over, Lug spared Bres in return for some information about agricultural techniques. The Mórrígan finished off the story by declaring victory for the Tuatha Dé Danaan and predicting the end of the world.

HOW DID A PROPHECY PICK IRELAND'S NEXT LEADER?

The conquests of Ireland didn't stop with the Tuatha Dé Danaan. They were themselves invaded by the Milesians, the sons of Míl, also known as the Gaels.

Míl came from Galicia in northwest Spain. His full name was Miles Hispaniae (Latin for "soldier of Spain"). His wife was named Scota ("Irishwoman"). A druid named Caichér had predicted that Míl's descendants would rule Ireland, and they did.

Míl himself didn't go to Ireland, but his sons did. The Milesians arrived in Ireland sometime after the Tuatha Dé Danaan had established themselves, perhaps between 350 and 250 B.C.E. They landed in southwest Ireland during the Feast of Beltane and fought an epic battle with the Tuatha Dé Danaan. They proceeded to Tara and clinched their hold on the country.

After the battle, a poet named Amhairghin divided Ireland between the two parties. The Milesians got the part that was aboveground, and the Tuatha Dé Danaan got the underground. The defeated Tuatha Dé Danaan retreated to the hills and mounds to become the fairy people.

HOW DID A WHITE BULL START A WAR?

Set around the first century B.C.E. the *Táin Bó Cuailnge* (toyn boe cooley), or the Cattle Raid of Cooley, is one of the most fabulous epic stories to come out of ancient Ireland. The oldest manuscript that records it is the *Book of Leinster*, written in the twelfth century. The Táin is part of the body of stories known as the Ulster Cycle. The story concerns the conflict between Ulster and Connacht, and the question of whether men can accept a female ruler.

One night, Ailill (Ahl-il), the king of Connacht, and his wife, Queen Medb (mayv), lay in bed arguing over which one of them was richer. Ailill suggested that Medb had improved her lot by marrying him and that it was proper for a man to rule the kingdom instead of her, but Medb insisted that she was as rich and tough as any king. They couldn't agree, so that very night they did an inventory. They laid out their garments and jewelry and lined up the livestock. And for every possession Ailill put up, Medb put up one just as good, except for one thing: a beautiful, white-horned bull.

IRISH BLESSING

May the road rise to meet you.

May the wind be always at your back.

May the sun shine warm upon your face.

And rains fall soft upon your fields.

And until we meet again,

May God hold you in the hollow of His hand.

This bull had been born to one of Medb's cows, but it had left her herd because it didn't want to belong to a woman. Medb was devastated, and she decided then and there that she would get a bull to equal the white-horned one. The only bull as good as this one was the brown bull of Cuailnge, the property of Daire mac Fiachna, king of Ulster.

Medb sent messengers to Ulster requesting the loan of the brown bull for one year. She offered generous terms: fifty yearling heifers, a large piece of land, a fabulous chariot, and her own "friendly thighs." Daire agreed readily, but that evening Medb's messengers boasted that if he had not accepted her terms, they would have taken the bull by force. After that, the deal was off.

Medb wasn't particularly perturbed by this; she had expected this to happen and quickly assembled a vast army. It marched off to Ulster to capture the brown bull.

The Ulster army started marching to meet its attackers, but on the way the soldiers were all struck by strange, debilitating pains, the result of an old curse by the goddess Macha. So instead of encountering an army, Medb's warriors met a single hero: Cuchulain (koo-HOOL-n).

WHO WAS THE CELTIC ACHILLES?

Cuchulain was the Celtic Achilles. He was seventeen years old, handsome, and utterly fearless. He had grown up as a foster son of King Conchobar (KONN-r) of Ulster. Cuchulain's name means "Culann's hound." He got this name because when the hound of Culann the smith attacked him, he killed it with his bare hands. Culann was upset because his watchdog was dead, and Cuchulain offered to do the job himself until he found a replacement canine.

When Cuchulain met the army from Connacht, he killed 100 soldiers single-handed. Next, he fought a series of Medb's warriors in single combat; Medb had persuaded soldiers to fight for her by bribing them with anything from land, to her own daughter in marriage, to her own thighs, which she had previously offered in exchange for the brown bull. Her warriors found these rewards enticing enough, but Cuchulain defeated all of them.

Turning back toward Ulster, Cuchulain discovered Medb's forces leading away the brown bull. He killed the leader, but the rest escaped with the bull, much to Cuchulain's distress. He took to his bed and slept for three days and nights, while the god Lug (who happened to be his father) healed his wounds.

While Cuchulain slept, the army of Ulster fought Medb's forces. The Ulster side was winning, but in the process lost 150 soldiers. When Cuchulain woke up and heard about this, he was furious and was transfigured by the warp-spasm, a battle-rage that turned him into the most fearsome sight anyone had ever seen. Possessed by this rage, he slaughtered hundreds of warriors, women, children, horses, and dogs. No man from Connacht escaped uninjured, but Cuchulain came away without a scratch.

Cuchulain was a fearsome opponent, but Medb finally came up with a way to get the best of him. She forced him to fight his foster brother, Fer Diad, whom Cuchulain loved more than any other man. She persuaded Fer Diad to fight on her behalf by promising him her daughter as a wife. The men fought for three days without either one gaining an advantage, and each one sent assistance to the other at night. On the fourth day, though, Cuchulain killed Fer Diad with the *gae bolga*, a frightful weapon that would expand into twenty-four barbs within a wound, like an exploding shell. Then Cuchulain sang a lament over his fallen friend.

The Ulster forces pursued Medb's army all the way to the border of Connacht. There, Cuchulain met Medb face-to-face and chose to spare her because she was a woman. But the conflict wasn't over.

Medb had sent the brown bull straight to Connacht to keep it safe. As soon as it arrived, it bellowed three times. The white-horned bull heard it and came racing to defend his territory. All the warriors watched this mighty duel, which lasted into the night and ranged over the entire island of Ireland.

In the morning, the brown bull reappeared, carrying the dead white-horned bull on his horns. He galloped back to Ulster, scattering bits of his enemy's flesh as he went. When he arrived at the border of Cuailnge, his heart broke and he died. Medb and Ailill made peace with Cuchulain and the men of Ulster, and there was no fighting between them for the next seven years.

Truce or no, Medb spent the years of peace scheming to get revenge on Cuchulain. During the cattle-raid wars, he had killed a man named Cailidín, who had six children. Medb sent off Cailidín's children to study sorcery. When they returned, she got them to make Cuchulain think that all of Ulster was overrun by invading armies. Deceived, Cuchulain prepared to go to battle.

Conchobar feared some trickery and sent Cuchulain to the Valley of the Deaf, where he wouldn't be able to hear the fake battle cries. The children of Cailidín redoubled their efforts to convince Cuchulain that battle was nigh, and Babd, one of the girls (and also a goddess of war), went to the hero in the shape of his mistress and asked him to fight the men of Ireland. Cathbad the druid and Cuchulain's real mistress tried to tell him that he had been bewitched, but he went off to fight anyway.

WHY DOES THE NAME DEIRDRE MEAN "SADNESS" OR "SORROW"?

Conchobar, king of Ulster, was not a pleasant character, especially not with his wife Deirdre, whom he met back in the days before the big cattle raid. Before Deirdre was born, Cathbad the druid predicted that she would be very beautiful but would bring ruin on the kingdom of Ulster. Conchobar liked the sound of the beautiful part, so he hid her away, intending to marry her when she was grown.

Deirdre grew up alone, away from the court. One day she saw her foster mother skinning a calf in the snow and a black raven drinking its blood. She said that she would like a husband with hair as black as a raven, cheeks red as blood, and a body white as snow. As it happened, just such a man lived nearby: Naoise, son of Uisneach.

Deirdre and Naoise got together and ran away to Scotland. They lived at the Scottish court for a while, but the Scottish king began to want Deirdre for himself, so they returned to Ireland. There, Naoise was killed by Conchobar's ally Eoghan mac Durthacht, and Deirdre went to Conchobar's court.

She spent a year there, never smiling or lifting her head from her knee. One day Conchobar asked her what she hated most, and she replied "you and Eoghan." Conchobar wickedly then decided to give

her to Eoghan. As she was riding in a chariot with both men, she leaped
out of the chariot and smashed her head to pieces on a giant rock.

HOW CAN SUCKING YOUR THUMB LEAD TO BOUNDLESS KNOWLEDGE?

Fionn mac Cumhaill, or Finn MacCool, was a great warrior and a major
hero of ancient Ireland. His stories come from the Duanaire Finn (the
"Lays of Finn"), part of the Fenian Cycle. Scholars have long debated
whether Finn was a real historical figure from the third century C.E.,
but the current consensus is that he was completely mythical.

Finn was the son of Cumhaill, king of Leinster; he served the high
king Conn, who reigned at Tara. Cumhaill was head of the Fianna, an
elite band of warriors. Men seeking admission to this band had to pass
a test of skill, such as fending off six men with spears, armed only with
a shield and a stick. All members had to swear an oath of allegiance to
the high king. If one of the Fianna was killed, the dead man's relatives
were supposed to let the Fianna avenge him.

After Cumhaill refused an order to attend a meeting at Tara, Conn
declared war on him. While he was getting ready to fight, Cumhaill
met Muirne, the daughter of a druid, and got her pregnant. Her outraged father vowed that Cumhaill would die in battle.

Cumhaill told Muirne to run away and hide someplace where
she could raise the baby in safety. Another druid had foretold that
this child, Finn, would be a great leader of the Fianna, and Cumhaill

wanted to make sure that this came to pass. Then he died, slain by the king's ally Goll mac Morna.

Muirne fled to a cave and gave birth to Finn, who grew up vowing revenge on Goll mac Morna and all his clan. Finn went to study with a druid named Fionn. Fionn was perpetually searching for the salmon of knowledge, a fish that would bring boundless knowledge to whoever ate it. One day, Finn caught the fish and went to cook it for Fionn. A blister rose up on its skin, and he pressed it down with his thumb. He then put his thumb in his mouth to soothe the burn, and he realized that he suddenly knew everything. From then on, whenever Finn didn't know something, he would suck his thumb, and all would be revealed to him.

Finn became leader of the Fianna. The Fianna loved the woods and wild animals. They cooked their meals in ovens of the Fianna, small, circular holes lined with stones and surrounded by low stone walls. (You can still find these all over Ireland.) Finn had two hounds that were actually his own nephews. His wife was a deer-woman from the otherworld. She raised their son Ossian (USH-een) in the wilderness; he grew up to be the poet of the Fianna and was a famous bard. (The stories about Finn are sometimes called the Ossianic Cycle because Ossian supposedly composed them.)

Finn and the Fianna had many magical adventures. They encountered ghosts and witches but always escaped with their lives. They got magical weapons from a giant with three arms, one foot, and an eye in the middle of his forehead; he was a fabulous blacksmith who could make blades fiercer than any made by humans.

When Finn was an old man, he got engaged to a beautiful young woman named Gráinne. She didn't want to marry him, so she cast a spell on Diarmait, the handsomest of the Fianna. Diarmait and Gráinne ran away together and lived happily for a while.

One day, all the Fianna went to hunt the magic boar of Beann Ghulban. This boar had been Diarmait's foster brother, and a prophecy said that it would cause his death. Sure enough, the boar gored Diarmait and ripped open his belly. The only way to save his life was for Finn to bring him a drink of water in his hands. Finn went and got the water, but then he remembered how Diarmait had stolen Gráinne away from him, and he let it trickle out through his fingers. Diarmait died, and the god Oenghus took his body away to Brú na Bóinne, where he was buried in a Newgrange tomb.

PART 4

Christianity on
Celtic Shores

The early Middle Ages in Europe are often called the Dark
Ages. But in Ireland, this period was a Golden Age, at least
for Christian monks. The Irish Christians lived a peaceful
existence, devoted to scholarship and prayer. A group of Irish
monasteries became a destination for scholars from all over
the Continent; they produced a body of astonishingly beautiful works of art and preserved classical learning for posterity.

It's impossible to understand the spread and the importance of Christianity in Ireland without examining the lives
of the men and women who made it their life's work to teach
others about their new faith—the lives of the Irish saints.
We don't know what actually happened and what was added
by imaginative storytellers. But that's no reason to dismiss
the stories of saints as pure fancy. How much do you know
about Ireland's saintly citizens and the Christian tradition
they inspired on the Emerald Isle?

WHO WAS ST. PATRICK?   .

Irish tradition credits St. Patrick with bringing Christianity to the Irish and transforming the island from a wild warrior society to a peaceful, scholarly kingdom. Not much is known about his life, or whether he existed at all. Most of what modern scholars know about the historical Patrick comes from his "Confession," an autobiographical sketch he (supposedly) wrote toward the end of his life. Patrick never mentions dates, so any dates that scholars claim for his deeds are just guesses.

Patrick's family was of British Celt (Briton) ancestry, and had lived in Britain for several centuries. His father was a well-to-do landowner, and Patrick probably grew up as a privileged young man, waited on by servants and educated in the classical tradition as it survived in Britain at the end of the Roman Empire. His family was Christian; his father was a deacon and his grandfather a priest.

Young Patrick was not a pious youth. By his own account, he had turned his back on the Christian god, and he committed some serious, unknown crime in his mid-teens.

When Patrick was almost sixteen, he was captured by a group of Irish slave traders and sold into slavery in Ireland. Patrick spent the next six years herding sheep alone in the hills, hunger and cold his constant companions. In his desolation, he turned to God and prayed constantly.

One day God spoke to Patrick, telling him that a ship was ready to take him away from Ireland. The problem was, the ship was not nearby, but in fact 200 miles away. Patrick set off on foot over the countryside, taking a great risk by running away from his master. He had no idea what he was headed for, but Patrick had no fear.

He reached the coast and found a ship ready to set sail. He asked the captain if he could sail with them, and the captain brusquely refused. So Patrick started to pray. Before he had finished his prayer, the sailors called him back and said he could sail with them.

The ship sailed for three days and then landed; it's not clear where. Patrick reports that he and the sailors wandered "in a desert" for twenty-eight days, but there's no place three days' sail from Ireland that matches that description. Some scholars have suggested that they landed in Gaul (modern France) after it was ravaged by barbarians in 407; others think it more likely that they were making circles around Britain.

IRISH PROVERB

A trout in the pot is better than a salmon in the sea.

In any case, they had nothing to eat. The captain turned to Patrick and asked him what his Christian god could do for them. Patrick admonished him, telling him to put his faith in God and ask Him for food. Sure enough, a whole herd of pigs came running across their path. The sailors killed and cooked a few, and their problems were solved.

Eventually, Patrick got back to his parents, who were overjoyed to see him after so many years and begged him never to leave them again. But Patrick discovered that home wasn't home anymore; he had changed too much in the last few years to feel comfortable resuming his life as a British landowner.

One night he dreamed about a man named Victoricus, whom he had known in Ireland. Victoricus gave him a letter entitled "The Voice of the Irish." At the same time, Patrick heard the voices of Irish people calling him back to them. He knew that Ireland would be his destiny.

He left home again and studied for the priesthood. Patrick struggled with his coursework. His education had been interrupted by his abrupt enslavement when he was a teenager, and he never made up the ground he had lost. In his later writings, he often lamented that his Latin was not very good and that he was uneducated. But he managed to learn the required material and was ordained.

Now a priest, Patrick went back to Ireland as its bishop, one of the first Christian missionaries in history; the traditional date for this journey is 432. The Irish were still barbarians, worshiping Celtic gods, raiding one another's cattle, and abducting slaves. Patrick was genuinely concerned about these problems. He found slavery to be particularly bad for women (his respect and concern for women made him very unusual among early medieval leaders).

Patrick was incredibly successful. He converted thousands of Irish to Christianity, established monasteries, and ordained priests all over the island. He placed bishops next to local kings, both to improve the Church's position with the Irish and to have someone to keep an eye on the worst raiders and warriors. By the end of his life, the Irish had stopped their endless tribal warfare and the slave trade had ended.

Converting the Irish wasn't always easy. As the Romans left Britain, local British kings grabbed the abandoned territory and took over the piracy trade. One British king named Coroticus attacked in the northern part of Ireland and killed or carried off thousands of recent converts. Patrick sent some priests to Coroticus to ask for the return of his people, but the king only laughed at them. Patrick responded with his "Letter to Coroticus," one of the two pieces of writing he left behind, in which he took the king to task for visiting this horror on his people. He also excommunicated him from the Christian faith, the worst punishment a priest could inflict on a believer. Patrick knew firsthand what it meant to be a slave, and his genuine love of his flock and grief at their suffering comes through in his prose quite clearly.

DID PATRICK REALLY CHASE THE SNAKES FROM IRELAND?

Over time, Patrick developed into a legendary figure. As the patron saint of Ireland and founder of Irish Christianity, he has been credited with numerous deeds. Here are a few of them:

* He banished snakes from Ireland—standing on top of Croagh Patrick, a hill in County Mayo, he rang a bell, and all the snakes in Ireland fled.
* He used the Irish shamrock, a three-leafed clover, to teach his converts about the Trinity, the one-in-three union of God, Jesus, and the Holy Spirit.
* He argued with High King Laoghaire at Tara and won for the side of Christianity.
* He was on speaking terms with both God and an angel, and once climbed Croagh Patrick to speak with God.
* He wrote the lovely prayer known as "Saint Patrick's Breastplate."

None of these myths can be verified, at least not as they are described today. For people who would credit Patrick with chasing the snakes from the Emerald Isle, it appears that the story was concocted approximately 300 years after his death. It is possible, however, that *snakes* was a metaphor for *pagans*. In addition, the shamrock story appeared centuries after Patrick's death, and the "Breastplate" was probably written in the seventh or eighth century. It is possible that Patrick did face down a king over some issue of Christianity, but probably not as it is told in the famous story about Laoghaire.

WHAT IS ST. BRIGID'S CONNECTION TO LEPROSY?

Brigid of Kildare was one of Patrick's converts to Christianity. She became abbess of a huge monastery that admitted both men and women. Some historians say she was actually a bishop. Most of what we know about St. Brigid is not historical fact, but it is fairly certain that Brigid was an immensely powerful woman who did a lot to advance Christianity in Ireland.

Brigid's father was an Irish nobleman. She converted to Christianity while still living with her parents. The first thing she did was to start handing out her father's food and goods to beggars. Her father was furious; he tossed her into his chariot and drove off to see the king of Leinster, to offer him Brigid as a wife.

When they got to the king of Leinster's palace, Brigid's father went in alone to see him. Out of respect, he first took off his sword and left it in the chariot with Brigid. While her father was in the castle negotiating her marriage, a leper came up to Brigid and asked her for help. The only thing available was her father's sword, so she gave him that. Her father and the king of Leinster then came back out. Of course, her father immediately noticed his sword was gone and wanted to know what Brigid had done with it. When he found out, he flew into a rage and beat her.

The king of Leinster, intrigued by this unusual young woman, stopped her father from hitting her and asked her why she gave away his things. She replied that if she could, she would steal all the king's wealth and give it away to the poor. Not surprisingly, the king decided not to marry her.

HOW DID ST. BRIGID OFFEND THE CATHOLIC CHURCH?

Brigid's monastery was huge; it contained a school of art and a scriptorium that produced gorgeous religious manuscripts. Brigid never abandoned her desire to help the poor, and her monastery was famous for its hospitality. After her death it turned into a center of pilgrimage, almost as big as a city. It became a place of refuge for anyone in Ireland, where people fleeing invaders could find safety and where kings could store their treasures.

Brigid was a radical in more ways than one. She admitted both men and women to her monastery, and she seems to have performed all the duties of a priest. This was an outrage for the Catholic Church, which has never approved of female leadership, though people broke many rules in far-flung Ireland in the early medieval days.

Brigid is sometimes called the Mary of the Gael. In one legend, she shaped a cross out of reeds to teach people about Christianity, much like St. Patrick used the shamrock to explain the Trinity. Today, Irish people still keep St. Brigid's crosses.

Brigid's feast day is celebrated on February 1, which is also the date of the Celtic feast of Imbolc, dedicated to the Irish fertility goddess Brigid. Coincidence? Certainly not—the Irish incorporated many aspects of their pagan Celtic religion into their version of Christianity. Another pagan-Christian combo associated with Brigid was St. Brigid's fire, which was lit in ancient times and kept burning into the Middle Ages.

HOW MANY PEOPLE DID COLUMCILLE CONVERT TO CHRISTIANITY?

Columcille, usually called Columba by non-Irish writers, converted thousands of Celts to Christianity and founded a plethora of monasteries. But he didn't do this simply out of love of God; he committed some serious sins and then threw himself into God's work as a form of atonement. Part of his penance was permanent exile from Ireland, which turned out to be the key to his impressive missionary accomplishments.

Columcille's real name was Crimthann, which means "fox" in Irish. He was the son of a nobleman of the Conaill clan, and was well educated in his youth. When he had finished his secular education, he went to study with Bishop Finian in Clonard, Gaul.

Finian owned a beautifully decorated Psalter, and Crimthann fell in love with it. He wanted to copy it, but Finian wouldn't let him. So Crimthann stole into the darkened church at night and copied it in secret. He had no candle, but the fingers of his left hand shone with lights to illuminate his work. Sadly for Crimthann, he got caught, and King Diarmait (or Dermot) made him give the copy back to Finian.

Crimthann became a monk and took the name Columcille ("Dove of the Church"). He made a pilgrimage to the grave of St. Martin of Tours, a legendary founder of monasteries. Inspired by Martin's work, he returned to Ireland and began founding monasteries right and left. By the time he was forty-one, he had founded forty-one monasteries.

But Columcille wasn't a good, peace-loving Christian. King Diarmait had one of Columcille's followers killed, and Columcille got angry; he persuaded all his warrior relatives to go fight the king. They defeated Diarmait, and Columcille took this opportunity to reclaim the Psalter he had copied from Finian years earlier. It was thereafter called the *Cathach* ("warrior").

But a monk is not supposed to go to war. Columcille was excommunicated and told that he must leave Ireland forever. Three thousand enemy soldiers had died in the conflict, and Columcille set himself a penance of converting 3,000 pagans to Christianity. With this daunting task ahead of him, Columcille enlisted twelve followers and sailed away to the island of Iona, off the coast of Scotland.

Columcille and his followers had embraced the White Martyrdom, the sacrifice of leaving behind the land they loved best and moving to an unknown territory, there to fast and do penance in a monastery they built. Soon, they found themselves unaccountably popular. People from all over Ireland, Scotland, and Britain heard about this new monastery with the famous abbot, and they came to visit. Many of them decided to become monks themselves.

Columcille decided that Iona could only hold 150 monks. When too many men congregated on the island, he sent off groups of thirteen monks to found new monasteries elsewhere in Scotland. Would-be monks kept coming, so Columcille kept sending off new groups of monastery founders. By the time he died, his men had founded more than sixty monastic communities all over Scotland, and he had met his goal of 3,000 conversions many times over.

WHAT IRISH SAINT WAS A MISSIONARY TO EUROPE?

Columbanus was born in Leinster around 540. As a young man, he traveled to Ulster to study and then entered a monastery in Bangor, County Down. He worked and prayed there for twenty-five years.

Around 590, Columbanus and twelve companions went to Gaul to found a monastery there. He was so successful that he actually founded three: Annegray, Fontaines, and the important Luxeuil. He worked with the uncivilized barbarians living in the forest, trying to convert them to Christianity.

This went against the practice of the local bishops, who preferred to stay in larger towns and cities and preach to their local believers. The bishops disapproved of Columbanus and summoned him, but he refused to go; instead, he sent them a letter saying that they weren't doing their jobs. In Columbanus's opinion, a bishop ought to be out in the countryside trying to reach the pagans.

The bishops conspired with the queen Brunhild of Burgundy to have Columbanus deported. He and his followers went to Nantes to catch a ship back to Ireland, but it sank. Columbanus and four companions survived and headed for northern Italy. In the Alps, his German translator, Gall, got sick and refused to go on. Columbanus had a big fight with him, and then left him behind.

SAINTS GALORE!

You can't toss back a pint in Ireland without hitting a saint. Most towns and professions have their own patron saints who take a special interest in their affairs. For example, St. Mac Dara is patron saint of fishermen in the Aran Islands. Other saints became famous by founding monasteries or teaching other saints. St. Enda from the Aran Islands taught many holy men, including St. Ciaran. Others became famous for their miraculous deeds, great wisdom, courage, or their unbelievable love of discomfort.

By 612, Columbanus and his companions were in Bobbio (in Emilia-Romagna, Italy) There they built the first-ever Irish-Italian monastery. Columbanus spent the rest of his years writing outrageous letters to his fellow churchmen. He is best known to us through his extraordinary correspondence, written in impeccable Latin and thoroughly grounded in Scripture. He never stopped criticizing his colleagues, and he seemed to have had no sense of humility or respect for rank. He even sent letters of scathing criticism to two popes. Columbanus died in Bobbio in 615.

WHICH SAINT LIVED IN A TREE?

The answer is Kevin of Glendalough, a member of the royal house of Leinster. He was born around 498. As a boy, he was taught by three holy men, and when he grew up, he moved to Glendalough, County Wicklow, a spectacular site between two lakes in a valley surrounded by sheer cliff faces.

Kevin is said to have taken up residence in a tree. He was very close to the animals—once a bird even laid an egg in his hand. He later moved into a tiny cave called St. Kevin's Bed. He spent his days either standing naked in one of the frigid lakes or hurling himself naked into a patch of nettles.

Kevin's fame spread, and he soon had a number of followers who persuaded him to let them build a monastic community on the shore of one of the lakes. They got him to move out of his cave into a little stone hut that they built for him.

WHICH SAINT WASHED UP IN IRELAND AFTER A SHIPWRECK?

Declan brought Christianity to southeast Ireland in the fifth century. It's said that he was adrift at sea, praying, when a stone floated by with his bell and vestments. He vowed that he would land wherever the rock landed and would there find his resurrection. He and his stone washed ashore at Ardmore, County Waterford, and there his stone still sits on the beach today. It was said to cure the rheumatism of any believer (except a sinner) who could manage to crawl under it—a feat that would be difficult for anyone afflicted with that ailment.

WHICH ILLUMINATED MANUSCRIPT WAS NAMED AFTER A ST. CIARAN'S COW?

Ciaran (or Kieran) was born in Connacht in 512 and became famous for founding the great monastery of Clonmacnoise in County Clare. Clonmacnoise was exceedingly isolated—it was surrounded by bog and could only be reached by river or by walking along a ridge called the Pilgrim's Road. (Bogs notwithstanding, this is another beautiful site.) This monastery flourished for 600 years as an international center of learning. Its residents produced many illuminated manuscripts, including the *Book of the Dun Cow*, the earliest known manuscript in the Irish language. It was named after Ciaran's cow, which might have supplied the hide that bound it.

WHICH SAINT WAS KNOWN AS "THE NAVIGATOR"?

Brendan was a very popular saint in medieval Europe. According to legend, he set out with twelve disciples in search of the land promised to the saints. At Clonfert, County Galway, he founded a monastery around 512. His adventures along the way, which included an encounter with a crystal column on the ocean and a passage through a curdled sea, thrilled generations of people in Ireland and Europe.

WHAT MODERN HOLIDAY DID SAMHAIN INSPIRE?

Ireland is a long way from Rome. As a result, the Irish developed a form of Christianity that didn't follow Rome's rules to the letter. The Irish were much more open to different beliefs and more accepting of nonbelievers. They didn't set as much store in the infallible authority of the church fathers, and they were more willing to allow women a say in how things would be run.

COUNTRY OF STONE CROSSES

Some of the most beautiful reminders of Ireland's early Christians are the tall crosses they left all over the country. These stone crosses are distinguished by a ring that surrounds the intersection of the cross. The ring is thought to represent the sun, in an attempt to reconcile Christian beliefs with earlier sun worship. Many crosses are carved with Celtic designs.

Early Irish Christians built their religion on top of a pre-existing culture and set of religious beliefs. The Celtic gods and the druidic traditions were still present, and everywhere people looked they saw the prehistoric mounds that were supposedly inhabited by the old deities. People still celebrated the old festivals, but put a new Christian veneer on them. For example, Samhain turned into All Hallows' Eve, better known as Halloween; All Hallows' Eve and All Saints' Day are still celebrated by the modern Catholic Church.

WHAT WAS THREEFOLD MARTYRDOM AND WHY DID THE IRISH PRACTICE IT?

After St. Patrick introduced Christianity to Ireland, many new Christians in the fifth and sixth centuries wanted to show how dedicated they were to their new religion. Patrick had told them stories of early Christian martyrs, men and women who were thrown to lions or murdered for their faith in other glorious, horrible ways. But Ireland was now peaceful, and no one was persecuting Christians there. So how could an Irish person match that level of commitment? Ever resourceful, the Irish came up with an intriguing theory of the kinds of martyrdom available to them, now called the "threefold martyrdom":

* **Red Martyrdom:** Red because the martyr sheds blood for faith's sake—this is the conventional martyrdom by torture and death.
* **Green Martyrdom:** Leaving the comforts of home to live in some isolated spot in the wilderness, studying Scripture and communing with God.
* **White Martyrdom:** Leaving Ireland to lead a monastic life in some foreign land, the most extreme form of sacrifice.

For most serious Irish Christians, the Green Martyrdom was the most likely plan of action. They had read stories about Egyptian and Middle Eastern hermits who had lived alone in the wilderness, fasting and doing penance, and they decided to adopt this model for themselves. They gave up material pleasures; in return, they hoped for grace in the next life. But they didn't count on becoming the most popular phenomenon to hit Ireland in the early Middle Ages.

WHY WAS BEING A HERMIT DIFFICULT IN MEDIEVAL IRELAND?

One of the most notable features of medieval Ireland was its absence of cities. The Irish lived in the countryside, farming little plots of land and grazing their cattle, and they never settled down in large groups. In Europe, cities served as gathering places for educated people and as nuclei for cultural exchange. Bishops had their headquarters in cities and spent their time preaching to their local, relatively wealthy, urban flocks. In Ireland, monasteries began to serve this purpose, with predictably different results.

The earliest Irish monks went off to live by themselves as solitary hermits. But they didn't stay alone for very long. Word got out about their wonderful isolation and asceticism, and people with their own aspirations toward monasticism came and asked to become their students.

Before long, solitary ascetics became the heads of small communities. These groups built themselves little enclosures containing huts for the monks, churches for believers to hear Mass, and often libraries. Many monasteries also included guesthouses, where visitors could stay to learn about Christianity and pray with the monks or nuns. The hospitality of Irish monasteries was famous; visitors were always welcome, and monks and abbots were always willing to baptize new believers.

Monasteries actually looked like small towns. Many of them contained a number of small buildings surrounded by a wall. The most distinctive type of architecture from this period was a kind of hut shaped a little like a beehive, constructed of stones held together without mortar. The skill necessary for building one of these was extraordinary, because the technique required balancing all the rocks perfectly; the monks grew so good at this job that some of their beehive huts remain standing today.

WHY DIDN'T MEDIEVAL MONKS GET MUCH SLEEP?

Medieval monastics' primary purpose was to worship, and worship they did—several times a day! The following is an outline of the traditional monastic services, or "offices":

* Matins, sung before daybreak (in the middle of the night)
* Lauds, sung at sunrise
* Prime, sung at about 6 A.M.
* Terce, sung at 9 A.M.
* Sext, sung at noon
* Nones, sung at 3 P.M.

- ♣ Vespers, sung at sunset
- ♣ Compline, sung right after Vespers

Monks had to get up twice in the night to walk over to the chapel and sing their offices. They complained about it, but that was the point—monastic life was supposed to include some suffering. But there was some reward even for people dragged out of their beds at midnight in midwinter—their prayer services were often done musically. The monastic offices are the origin of the famous Gregorian chants, beautiful a cappella musical arrangements of psalms and other pieces of Scripture.

WHY DID THE IRISH LEARN LATIN?

Latin, the language of the former Roman Empire, became the language of the Christian church. All religious documents and correspondence, including the Bible, were written in Latin, and the Mass was performed in Latin. The Irish monks who entered the Church in the sixth century spoke the Irish language, but all of them had to learn Latin in order to write.

The Irish had to start from scratch in learning their new language. New Christians in other parts of Europe had been in contact with the Romans and their traditions and often knew the basics of Latin; French and Spanish are largely derived from it. But the Irish language is not closely related to Latin. The Irish needed a book that taught Latin starting with the absolute basics.

This was apparently the first time the problem had ever come up—there weren't any basic Latin grammars. So the Irish took on the task of producing one (generations of students of Latin have them to thank for their suffering). An obscure scholar named Asper took a grammar by the Latin grammarian Donatus and adapted it for the Irish market. This grammar, called the *Ars Asporii*, used a question-and-answer format to convey Latin sentence structure and vocabulary, but with an Irish monastic twist. The author removed all pagan terms and substituted the language of monastic life. The book was a huge success (for a Latin textbook), and by the seventh century it was established as a key authority.

ðo you speak ırısh?

The Irish language is just one of many Celtic languages. Irish comes from the Celtic branch called *Goidelic*, which also includes Scots Gaelic. The term *Goidelic* comes from the Irish Celts' name for themselves, *Goídil*, which gives us the modern word "Gaelic." Irish is not closely related to the languages spoken nearby, particularly Welsh and Breton (spoken in Brittany, France), but instead had its roots in Spain; hence, scholars think the ancestors of the Irish came from Spain.

WHAT WERE THE DUTIES OF MONASTIC STUDENTS?

One of the most important functions of monasteries was education, and monastic schools were well attended (mostly by boys). Some of the students were treated as foster children by the monks, living in the care of another family until they were ready to return to their homes and assume adult responsibilities. Many noble warrior fathers seem to have thought that their sons would be safer in a monastery than at home. Students had to find and prepare food for the monks and help out with the business of running the monastery. But most of their time was spent studying and working.

IRISH PROVERB

Drink is the curse of the land.
It makes you fight with your neighbor.
It makes you shoot at your landlord—
and it makes you miss him!

By the sixth century, Irish schools had a firm curriculum. Students studied Latin grammar, biblical exegeses, and the ecclesiastical calendar. A monastery's library contained several basic texts, including the Bible (the Latin Vulgate, translated by St. Jerome), various commentaries on Scripture, Jerome's book on early church writers called *De viris illustribus*, and a church history by Eusebius.

The computation of the ecclesiastical calendar was of special interest to Irish monks and medieval religious scholars in general, and big monasteries stocked several works on the subject. The seventh-century scholar Columbanus mentioned calendrical problems in several of his letters.

HOW DID IRISH MONKS GET CARPAL TUNNEL SYNDROME?

In the days before photocopiers and scanners, the only way people could copy a book was the hard way—by hand. Every book at a monastery, from the Bible to the textbooks used in the schools, had to be hand-copied. This took up much of the monks' time. Monasteries lent books to one another for the purpose of copying; often the borrowing monastery would make two copies, one for itself and one for the lending monastery.

The early monks didn't write on paper, but on parchment, which is made of dried sheepskin. The most important texts sometimes got transcribed on vellum, which is made from dried calfskin.

The Irish monks, copying away in their monasteries, didn't realize that their work would have lasting implications for all of European history. But they did, in fact, preserve classical learning for posterity. After the Roman Empire fell, the state of education fell along with it. The Romans and the Greeks were consummate scholars and wrote learned treatises on all manner of topics—history, science, and literature. In the early medieval period, much of that literature was in danger of being lost forever. People on the Continent didn't know its importance, and many of them were too busy fighting barbarians, or becoming barbarians themselves, to worry about literary matters. In Ireland, though, peace prevailed.

The Irish monks even transcribed their own local epics in Irish. These texts, including Irish epics such as the *Táin Bó Cuailnge*, are some of the earliest examples of vernacular literature.

WHAT ARE ILLUMINATED TEXTS?

The Irish monks weren't content to simply copy texts. They embellished them to make them into works of art. They were fascinated with the shapes of letters and experimented with ways of making them more beautiful. They invented a script called Irish miniscule that was easier to read and write than many other medieval scripts had been; it was so successful that monasteries across Europe adopted it.

IRISH BLESSING
Leave the table hungry.
Leave the bed sleepy.
Leave the table thirsty.

Monks also used color and drawings to decorate their texts, in a technique called illumination. They took their inspiration from ancient Celtic art, the spirals and zigzags that decorated the tombs at Newgrange and myriad metal objects. Using paints made from various pigments, including insects, they applied brilliant colors to their complicated drawings to create books that would dazzle the eye of the reader. Letters themselves became fabulously embellished; sometimes an entire page would be filled with an intricately decorated single letter. Some artists even adorned their pages with gold leaf that caught the light and literally "illuminated" the text.

Ireland is home to several famous illuminated books that survive today:

* The *Book of Kells*
* The *Book of Armagh*
* The *Book of Durrow*
* The *Book of Dimma*

Each of these is a masterpiece by the standards of any day, full of illustrations and text painstakingly planned and executed.

WHAT'S SO SPECIAL ABOUT THE *BOOK OF KELLS*?

The *Book of Kells* is probably the most famous illuminated manuscript in the world. Its several volumes contain the four gospels and supplemental texts. Its fame is due to the extraordinary art that graces almost every one of its pages.

The history of the *Book of Kells* is murky and full of legend, but the most common story says that it was written around 800 at St.

Columcille's monastery on Iona, off the coast of Scotland. Vikings started hitting the monastery at about this time, and the monks fled with the book to Kells in Ireland. The first written reference to the book is a report from the year 1007, noting that the great "Gospel of Columkille" had been stolen and found soon after, buried in the ground. At some point, the metal shrine containing the book disappeared, perhaps stolen by Vikings. Along the way, the book lost about thirty of its folios.

In 1661, the *Book of Kells* ended up at Trinity College in Dublin. It wasn't always cared for properly and was occasionally mistreated. In the eighteenth century, a bookbinder actually trimmed its pages, which caused irreparable damage. It was rebound in four volumes in 1953. Its modern keepers have been much more diligent about protecting it from light and moisture, and keep it in strictly controlled conditions. Astonishingly, given all the book has been through, it is still mostly intact, and the colors are still bright.

Today, the people of Kells want their book back. The librarians at Trinity College aren't sure that it would be cared for properly, but they have considered the possibility of returning the book to its medieval home. Meanwhile, it still resides in Dublin.

How did the Vikings end Ireland's Golden Age?

Medieval Ireland became known as the Island of Saints and Scholars. Irish monasteries such as Glendalough and Clonmacnoise were famous all over Europe, luring students from England and the Continent. Clonmacnoise in County Offaly was known as the University of the West. But it didn't last.

Beginning in 795, Viking raiders started coming to Ireland. They weren't interested in learning or art, but they knew where to find riches—in monasteries. Over the next 200 years, Vikings attacked and burned hundreds of monasteries and killed countless monks. Ireland's Golden Age was coming to an end.

Still, the Irish remember their medieval Christian forebears and their glorious heyday. They have carefully preserved the relics of that day, the exuberant decorated texts, and works in metal. People travel from all over the world to visit Irish shrines and holy sites. And the world still has access to classical texts, which would not have been possible if Ireland had not created a group of joyful, imaginative scholars and an age of peace.

PART 5

The Rise of the Vikings

Early medieval Ireland was a site of battles, deadly rivalries, and relentless invasions. While monks led secluded lives in their monasteries, Irish lords vied for rule of the island. When the Vikings arrived, some Irish lords fought against them, but others took the Vikings' side. It was in the midst of this complicated situation that the great hero Brian Boru emerged. How much do you know about the Vikings and one of Ireland's greatest heroes?

HOW DID THE ROCK OF CASHEL GET ITS NAME?

Ireland in its early days of Christianity was still ruled by the same Celtic noble families as before; the difference was that now they were Christian. Their new religion, however, didn't stop the old traditions of tribal warfare and cattle stealing. Irish historians used to claim that the tribal societies of pre-Viking Ireland had strict rules for warfare that limited the damage of conflicts, and that the Vikings ruined this state of relative peace. Historical evidence, though, indicates that the Irish were at least as violent and prone to ravage the countryside as their invaders.

The most powerful family during this period was the Eóghanacht, who had occupied the plain of Munster by the seventh century. Their home base was at the Rock of Cashel, in County Tipperary. "Cashel" is an Anglicized version of the Irish *caiseal*, which means "fortress"; it got this name because Cashel is a high hill covered with fortifications. (Cashel rivaled Tara as a seat of power during the medieval period.)

STEADY AS A ROCK

Legend says that St. Patrick converted Aengus, leader of the Eóghanacht, at the Rock of Cashel, so it's known as St. Patrick's Rock. The Rock of Cashel is now a popular tourist site.

To the east of Munster lay Laigin, which became the modern province of Leinster. To the north lay the kingdom of Ulaid, which became Ulster. In the center was Meath, which was overtaken by members of the Uí Néill clan, the ancestors of the modern O'Neills. To the west was Connacht, named after a relative of the Uí Néills, Conn Cétchatchach; this province was dominated by the Uí Briúin clan. The Uí Néills were particularly prolific; they eventually laid claim to all of Ireland and called their king the "high king."

Irish genealogy was anything but simple and clear. Kings took several wives and had many sons, thereby splitting royal families into several branches. These branches fought with one another and with outside enemies. Families rose and fell in power and there was no clear sense of national unity, whatever the Uí Néills might try to claim; there was no "Ireland" as such, only small kingdoms fighting and stealing one another's cattle.

WHY AREN'T A LOT OF CELTIC WORDS USED IN THE ENGLISH LANGUAGE?

After the Celts spread across central and western Europe, another group of people came in their wake. These were the Germanic people, who spoke a completely different language. They spread into the Baltic region, through northern Germany, Denmark, the Netherlands, and north into Norway and Sweden.

The people who lived in the southern part of that area spoke the Germanic languages, which eventually evolved into modern German dialects; the ones who lived in Scandinavia spoke Norse tongues, ancestors of modern Norwegian, Danish, and Swedish.

Around the time the Romans left Britain, the Germanic peoples started to cast longing gazes at the fertile island to their west. In 449 C.E., a whole passel of them got into their boats and sailed across the North Sea to Britain. Old English chronicles name them as the Angles, Saxons, and Jutes. They were fearsome people, eager for violence, and the native Britons (who were Celts) fled before their swords and fires. As they established themselves, people in Britain began to refer to them collectively as the Angles, or the English. This time in British history is known as the Anglo-Saxon period.

The Celts retreated to Wales, Cornwall, and Scotland, which, along with Ireland, are the few places that Celtic languages remain today. The invaders took over everything else, the most fertile parts of Britain. The extent to which they overwhelmed the natives is evident in the scarcity of Celtic words in the English language.

WHAT BATTLE TECHNIQUES DID THE VIKINGS USE TO SUBDUE IRELAND?

The Vikings were Scandinavian people from Norway, Sweden, and Denmark, basically a northern version of the earlier Germanic invaders. Between 750 and 1050, Scandinavians spread all over northern Europe and into the Atlantic, establishing colonies in faraway Iceland, Greenland, and even Labrador. They were collectively called Vikings, which either comes from the Norse word *vik*, meaning "bay," or the

Old English word *wic*, meaning "camp." Either is possible: Viking boats were often found in bays, and they set up camps across the western part of Europe.

The Vikings called themselves *Ostmen*, or "men from the east." They were excellent sailors, and they had a reputation for raiding, stealing, and burning whatever they found in their way.

The Vikings first hit Ireland in 795, landing their technologically advanced warships at Lambay Island near the site of modern Dublin. From there they launched attacks up and down the coast, first concentrating their raids on the northern and western seaboards. Between 820 and 840, they ventured down rivers into the interior of the island, attacking churches for booty and captives.

The Vikings developed a quick and efficient style of hit-and-run attack. Although the Irish fought back, the Vikings were at least as ferocious as the Celts and much better armed. Also, the Irish were never unified against the Vikings. The wealth of the monasteries attracted the attention of several Irish lords, and sometimes monks found themselves under attack by their own countrymen.

HOW DID THE MONKS PROTECT THEMSELVES FROM THE VIKING INVASION?

The monks responded by fortifying their monasteries, reinforcing wooden walls with stone, and adding other defensive structures. The most famous of these fortifications were round towers, tapering stone cylinders 100 feet high that doubled as bell towers and watchtowers; a five-story staircase led up to the top.

The entrances to these towers were high above the ground and could only be entered by climbing a ladder. When the monks were under attack, they could all climb into the tower and then pull up the ladder after themselves. Then they could climb up to the top and watch their monastery burn as they themselves slowly starved. Of course, they hoped the invaders would leave before that happened.

Did the Vikings really wear horned helmets?

Only in fiction. In the nineteenth century, northern Europeans developed a passion for their medieval ancestors, and they created all sorts of art and literature about the Vikings. The image of Vikings in picturesque helmets was invented during this period.

Why was Dublin built as a military town?

Eventually the Vikings stopped raiding and started settling down. They built settlements called *longphorts*, which were similar to naval camps. They used these encampments as bases for further attacks, but also as foundations for towns. The Vikings founded Dublin around

840, when they spent the winter moored there. The city's name comes from the words *Dubh Linn*, which mean "Black Pool." Dublin became the Vikings' chief base in Ireland, the place from which they launched raids on unconquered lands.

IRISh PROVERB

It's no use carrying an umbrella if your shoes are leaking.

One of the things that prevented the Irish natives from defending themselves against the Vikings' earliest onslaughts was the endless state of mild to severe warfare that they maintained against one another. They couldn't stop arguing among themselves long enough to join forces against their common invaders, nor did they have any sense of a single Irish nation.

As the Vikings became more settled, though, they became more vulnerable to attack—people without property have nothing to defend, but someone with a house and farm has to keep watch over them. Norse Vikings and Danish Vikings fought over the same Irish territory. Starting in about 850, Irish kings began to launch their own raids on the Vikings with some success. A funny thing happened around that time; Irish kings and Vikings started to form alliances to fight other Irish kings, who had their own Viking allies.

By 900, the Vikings' Irish administration (such as it was) had fallen into complete disarray, and the invaders had turned their attention to new raids in Iceland and northern Britain. This gave the Irish a window of opportunity, and they expelled the Vikings from Dublin in 902. Many Vikings left Ireland and bothered Britain instead for a few years.

Unfortunately, it was only a brief respite for the Irish. The Vikings came back in 914, took back Dublin, Munster, and Leinster, and spent another twenty years in power. After 950 they ceased to be much of a military threat, but they stayed on in the parts of Ireland that had become their home.

Despite the constant warfare, the reality is that most Irish people lived most of their lives just as they had before the Vikings arrived. In fact, some people lived better; the Vikings brought with them a number of valuable ideas from the mainland. They built the first Irish towns, they brought fancy boat-building techniques, and they could coin money. They used these skills to help increase trade to and from Ireland, which brought in artistic influences from the outside.

When the Vikings returned to Ireland in 914, they built a new stronghold at Dublin 2 miles closer to the sea than their earlier settlement; apparently, they wanted to be able to escape more quickly if necessary. They planned the city carefully, laying out streets and houses with great attention to detail. They even designed a rudimentary drainage system, which suggests the presence of a strong leader in charge of urban development. By the late tenth century, the Kingdom of Dublin was one of the most important political units in Western Europe.

HOW DID TRADE INTEGRATE THE VIKINGS INTO IRISH SOCIETY?

Thousands of people lived in Viking Dublin. There were merchants and craftsmen of all types—carpenters, shipwrights, blacksmiths, weavers, leather-workers, and others. Dublin's location put it right on the trade routes from Scandinavia down to England, and the Vikings traded vigorously with the people of England and continental Europe. They got wine, silver, and wool from England and Europe, which they sent on to Scandinavia. From Scandinavia they received amber, ivory, furs, and slaves, which they moved into European markets.

The Vikings also traded with the Irish people. This brought them into close contact with their new neighbors, and it appears that the two groups coexisted in relative harmony. (Some of those slaves traded by the Vikings did happen to be Irish, but the sad fates of a few individuals didn't necessarily hurt Viking–Irish relations on the whole; the Irish didn't all love one another.)

The Irish taught the Vikings about Christianity. Members of the two groups married one another and sent their children to be fostered in one another's homes. Scandinavian artistic styles appear in Irish art around this time, and some of Ireland's most "characteristic" metalwork patterns of interlaced spirals with free-flowing tendrils, sometimes incorporating the shapes of animals, date from this period.

HOW DID BRIAN BORU BECOME IRELAND'S HIGH KING?

The Vikings displaced some of the Irish chiefs who had held sway throughout the island. This allowed other Irish families to try to take their places. The most important of these families were the rulers of Dál Cais in the lower Shannon region, who took over the lands of the displaced Eóghanacht. In the first half of the eighth century, the Irish lord Cennétig, son of Lorcán, became king of north Munster, a region called Thomond; he died in 951.

Cennétig had two sons, Mathgamain and Brian. Mathgamain added east Munster to his kingdom, along with the Viking-controlled areas of Limerick and Waterford. He became known as king of Cashel. Mathgamain died in 976. His brother Brian succeeded him and became known as Brian Boru, the greatest of Ireland's high kings.

Brian was born around 941. His nickname, Boru, came from the old Irish word *bóruma*, which might have meant "of the cattle tribute." Or it might have come from the name of a fort in County Clare called Beal Boru.

Brian Boru was an excellent soldier. In 978 he led his warriors to victory in the Battle of Belach Lechta, in which the Dál Cais took the kingship of all of Munster from the Eóghanacht.

The rulers of other provinces took note of this; if Brian had all of Munster, he might want more territory. The high king of the Uí Néills, Máel Sechnaill, brought an army down to Munster and cut down the tree of Magh Adhair, a sacred tree on the Dál Cais family's royal inauguration site. This was a way of saying that the Uí Néills didn't recognize Brian's claim to the throne.

However, Brian refused to back down and quickly took over most of the southern half of Ireland. In 997, Brian met with Máel Sechnaill and the two kings agreed formally to divide Ireland between themselves. Brian got the south and the Uí Néills got the north.

But Brian wasn't content to stop there. In 1001, he defeated Máel Sechnaill and went about northern Ireland reinforcing his claim to it. In 1005, he went to Armagh and stayed at Emain Macha, the ancient capital of Ulster.

The problem with building an empire is that you can't watch your old territories while you're off conquering new ones. As Brian marched around, adding Ulster and other lands to his kingdom, Dublin and Leinster rebelled. He pushed them back in late 1013 and then fought a huge battle at Clontarf on April 23, 1014.

Soldiers came from the Isle of Man and other islands in the channel to help the rebel forces. Brian's army from Munster finally won, but Brian himself was killed. His followers took his body to Armagh, where they held a wake that lasted twelve days, and then buried him.

WHY WAS BRIAN BORU HAILED AS A NATIONAL HERO?

Many legends sprang up about the Battle of Clontarf. Later observers claimed that it was a battle between Irish and Viking invaders, with the king of the Irish winning a great victory for his nation and sacrificing his life in the process.

According to a popular version of the story written long after the event, Brian was too old to go to battle. While his soldiers fought, he knelt in his tent, praying with his Psalter. The Viking warrior Brodir ran into Brian's tent and hacked at the old king. An Irish boy named Tadhg raised his arm to protect Brian, but the Viking sliced through his arm and cut off Brian's head in the same stroke. The boy's wound healed instantly when Brian's blood touched it. This episode portrays the Vikings as monsters and glorifies Brian's heroic, patriotic sacrifice as leader of the Irish resistance.

Modern scholars think it more likely that the battle was an internal conflict; Vikings no doubt were involved, but simply as soldiers for one side or the other. Brian himself was married to a Viking woman and might have given his daughter to a Viking in marriage. The men of Leinster were allied with the Vikings of Dublin. Certainly, the Vikings didn't leave Ireland after the conflict; they were too thoroughly integrated into Irish society by that time. Most historians now say that the Battle of Clontarf, though it made for some lovely literary interpretations, actually wasn't very important and held no real political significance.

Brian's own family was severely disadvantaged after the battle, mainly because most of them had died in it. His descendants, the O'Briens, managed to hang on to some power in Munster, but they were definitely not in a position to claim the high kingship.

Brian turned into a national hero. Later, Irish Nationalists would hold him up as an example of an Irish leader defeating foreign forces. They saw the period between Brian's death and the Norman invasion under Strongbow in 1170 as an age when there were no foreigners in Ireland.

WHAT IS BRIAN BORU'S CONNECTION TO GUINNESS?

The Irish people still consider Brian Boru to be a great cultural hero. One of the images associated with him is the Brian Boru's Harp. It occupies a prominent place in everyday Irish culture—as the symbol of Guinness Stout and as the name of Guinness's lager, Harp. You can see the original harp in the Trinity College library, although it's unlikely that Boru ever actually owned it.

In addition, a number of sites are associated with Brian Boru.

- ♣ Boru is said to have studied at the monastery of St. Finan Lobhar in the Killarney region.
- ♣ Killaloe in County Clare is the site of Brian's castle Kincora and Beal Boru, or Boru's Fort.
- ♣ You can see his grave at Armagh's Church of Ireland Cathedral.
- ♣ Nenagh, County Tipperary, boasts the site where his soldiers killed 1,000 Leinster men.

WHAT REPERCUSSIONS DID BRIAN BORU'S VICTORY HAVE ON IRELAND?

Brian's victory did have some real repercussions for Ireland. The Uí Néills had lost their stranglehold on the high kingship, and though they recovered it occasionally over the next 150 years, the title itself had lost most of its meaning. Without the Uí Néills in power, the leadership of Ireland was an open question, and many men were ready to take the job for themselves.

Economic changes in this period actually made warfare more dangerous. People were growing more food and producing more resources than they had in earlier centuries, and consequently the population was increasing. Lords required their growing populations to pay dues of livestock and money, a situation similar to the feudal system in effect in England and Scotland. With the added resources and manpower, chiefs had the wherewithal to march farther afield and sustain longer campaigns, with accompanying higher fatalities.

To defend themselves, Irish lords built larger castles and fortifications. The kings of the provinces struggled against one another, but no one came out on top. Every time it looked as if one man would prevail, one of his so-called allies did something treacherous and it all came tumbling down.

By 1170, however, the question of an Irish high king was irrelevant. The Anglo-Normans had arrived, and from that point on Ireland's destiny was inextricably linked with that of the larger island to the east—England.

PART 6

Enter the British

Just as the Irish were beginning to see the emergence of truly powerful high kings, something happened that altered the course of their history forever—the Normans arrived. The Norman English, who had recently consolidated their rule over Britain, began a conquest that eventually led to English domination of Ireland.

WERE THE ENGLISH INVITED TO IRELAND?

The ironic thing about the Norman arrival is that an Irishman invited them in. Dermot MacMurrough, king of Leinster, was unseated from power in 1166 by Rory O'Connor, king of Connacht. MacMurrough had heard that the Norman (derived from the term "North man," descendants of earlier Vikings) knights over in England were particularly tough, so he asked his English neighbor King Henry II if he could borrow some of them to get his throne back. Henry, alert to the possibilities of the situation, sent over Richard FitzGilbert de Clare—known to the world as Strongbow.

MacMurrough had guessed right about one thing—the Norman knights were tough. In 1170 Strongbow and his team of heavily armored knights plowed through the relatively lightly armed forces of Irish lords. The Irish probably could have put up a good fight if they'd joined together. But Ireland at that time was divided up among 100 or more kings, who tended to wait in their home territories for the Normans to arrive. When they did, the result was invariably Norman victory.

What MacMurrough didn't expect, though, was that the Normans might like Ireland and want to stick around. MacMurrough allowed Strongbow to marry his daughter Aoife, and when MacMurrough died in 1171, Strongbow had himself declared lord of Leinster. No one in Ireland could afford to object.

But someone back in England wasn't happy about all this—the English king. Henry II watched Strongbow's string of successes and began to worry that his knight was getting too many ideas about his own power. So Henry sailed to Ireland to oversee the campaign and assert his own rights.

To consolidate the Norman victories, Henry declared Strongbow the king of Leinster but granted the province of Meath to Hugh de Lacy, a loyal knight. In 1175 Henry signed the Treaty of Windsor with Rory O'Connor, MacMurrough's old rival. The treaty declared O'Connor high king of Ireland, but it also said that he was a vassal of the king of England. Through these maneuvers, Henry established a system of competing lords in Ireland, who all ultimately owed their allegiance to the English Crown.

Over the next seventy years, Anglo-Norman knights extended English control over about three-fourths of Ireland. It wasn't so much an organized campaign as a series of advances by Norman adventurers who wanted their own fiefdoms. They only took property that they judged worth fighting for, so substantial portions of northwest Ulster and southwest Munster remained Irish.

The Irish probably thought they'd be able to take back their lands as soon as the Normans let down their guard, but the Normans did something the locals didn't expect—they built castles. Irish nobles generally moved around with their cattle, so they rarely built substantial structures. But the Normans immediately set their serfs to building *motte castles*—earthen mounds defended by ditches and wooden towers. The mounds from these motte castles still dot the Irish countryside. Once these were in place, they built more substantial castles out of stone.

HOW DID THE IRISH TAKE BACK THE COUNTRY?

Norman power in Ireland reached its peak around 1250 to 1275. After this, Irish lords began to reclaim their rights to the land. There were a number of reasons for this.

First, the definitions of Norman and Irish became vague. After Norman families had spent a few generations in Ireland, they had less and less in common with their cousins in England. Distinctions of loyalty and family allegiance became blurred as the descendants of Norman settlers began to think of themselves as Irish.

IRISH BLESSING

Here's to a long life and a merry one.
A quick death and an easy one.
A pretty girl and an honest one.
A cold beer and another one!

Another reason was the impact of foreign politics. England was constantly fighting with Scotland and mainland Europe, and the king demanded that the Norman-Irish lords contribute men and money. This weakened the power of the Norman-Irish lords.

In one instance, the English war with Scotland led to a direct attack by Scots on Normans in Ireland, when the Scot Edward Bruce invaded Ireland between 1315 and 1317. Although he didn't achieve any lasting conquests, his army inflicted such damage that many Norman towns did not recover for decades. His invasion also revealed to the Gaelic lords that the Normans were not unified.

The Irish kings took advantage of this Norman weakness. Starting from their strongholds in Connacht and Munster, they pushed Norman lords off their estates one by one. To improve the strength and discipline of their armies, the Irish lords hired tough mercenaries from Scotland called "gallowglasses." By the late fourteenth century, the Irish had regained much of their land.

The English king Richard II wasn't too happy about this. He personally led two reconquest expeditions in 1394–1395 and 1399, and he took back much of his lost territory. But the rebellion of Henry Bolingbroke (recounted in Shakespeare's *Richard II*) forced Richard to return home to England, where he eventually lost his throne and his life. With the English leadership gone, the Irish grabbed their property right back again.

For the next few decades, the English monarchs were too tied up in the War of the Roses to worry about Ireland, so the Irish lords continued to extend their power. By the early 1500s the area under English control had shrunk down to the city of Dublin and a small area surrounding it. This area of English influence was known as "the Pale."

BEYONÒ TbE PALE

The Irish Pale has given us the term "beyond the pale," which refers to actions or situations that are outside of what is normally accepted. For the English, going beyond the pale meant venturing into the strange and barbaric lands of Ireland.

WHY DID THE "LORD OF IRELAND" KILL IRELAND'S MOST POWERFUL FAMILY?

When Henry VIII became king of England in 1509, he also inherited the title "Lord of Ireland." English kings had carried this title for years without it meaning much. But, as people throughout Europe were to learn, Henry VIII was the kind of guy who liked to get his way.

The Norman-Irish lords had essentially been ruling themselves as independent monarchs for years. The most significant of these lords were the earl of Kildare and the earl of Desmond, both from the FitzGerald family (called the "Geraldine earls"), and the earl of Ormond from the Butler family. Garrett Og FitzGerald, earl of Kildare, served as lord deputy of Ireland for many years and was effectively the most powerful man on the island.

Henry VIII had three problems with Garrett Og: He was too powerful; his father had supported the York family's claim to the English throne over the Tudors; and he wasn't taking Henry's side in his fight with the pope on whether he could divorce Anne Boleyn. So Henry had Garrett Og thrown into the Tower of London.

"Silken" Thomas Lord Offaly, Garrett Og FitzGerald's son, started a largely symbolic rebellion in 1534 to show that Henry needed the support of the FitzGeralds to govern Ireland. Henry took the symbolism literally and sent over an army to set them in line. Thomas's supporters backed off, and soon the FitzGeralds surrendered on the condition that they receive mercy. Henry agreed, and then promptly had most of them killed. The loss of Ireland's most powerful family left a power gap that Henry promptly filled with his own supporters.

HOW DID HENRY VIII INITIATE NEARLY 500 YEARS OF RELIGIOUS UPHEAVAL IN IRELAND?

Religion added a new twist to the conflict in 1536, when the English parliament passed the Act of Supremacy. This made Henry the head of the Church of England and introduced the Protestant Reformation to the British Isles. England had been a Catholic country, but now it became officially Protestant. The Church of England was not especially different theologically from the Catholic Church, but it was different enough to provoke fights. Most important, Henry now refused to acknowledge the pope in Rome as the supreme leader on Earth; instead, Henry was now the head of his own church.

The Irish were still Catholic and wanted to stay that way. Although an Irish parliament officially recognized Henry as the head of their church in 1537, most Irish maintained allegiance to the pope—and considered this ample reason to take up arms. This was the start of religious violence that has plagued Ireland for nearly 500 years.

HOW DID ELIZABETH I SPARK "THE FLIGHT OF THE EARLS"?

Elizabeth I was an avowed Protestant. She spent much of her reign fighting with Catholic leaders in Rome and in Spain, who constantly tried to topple her from the English throne. Under these conditions, she couldn't allow Catholics to attack her from her own backyard, so she gave tacit approval for Protestant adventurers to go claim land in Ireland from Catholic landowners.

The Irish were still resisting Protestant rule. In 1579, James Fitz-Maurice FitzGerald, cousin to the earl of Desmond, went to the Continent and brought back a small army to oppose Protestant rule in Ireland. Elizabeth responded by sending over a bigger army of English soldiers, who broke up the Irish rebellion. She confiscated the earl of Desmond's lands, had most of his family put to death, and resettled his old estates with loyal English subjects.

Elizabeth's greatest Irish challenge came with the revolt of Hugh O'Neill, earl of Tyrone. The O'Neills were an old Irish family originally from Ulster who once had claims to the high kingship of Ireland. O'Neill appealed for help in his rebellion to the king of Spain, who sent more than 4,000 soldiers to help fight England. Spain was Elizabeth's greatest enemy, so she raised a massive army of 20,000 soldiers to crush the rebellion. In 1601 her army defeated the Hiberno-Spanish force at Kinsale.

O'Neill and his fellow Catholic earls tried to mount another attack, but they couldn't gather sufficient forces to have any chance of victory. In 1607 they fled Ireland in the "Flight of the Earls."

WHAT IS THE ULSTER PLANTATION?

James I became king of England, Scotland, and Ireland in 1603. He knew that O'Neill's strongest supporters had come from the north; Ulster at this time was the most Catholic and least Anglicized area of the island.

James I, therefore, decided to fix Ulster by settling it with loyal Protestants from England and Scotland, a plan that came to be known as the Ulster Plantation. The Protestant population he settled there developed on very different lines from the Catholic Irish in the south. This led to considerable difficulties during the Irish struggle for independence, and more recently, during the Troubles in Northern Ireland.

WHY DID THE BRITISH THINK THE IRISH WERE BARBARIC?

The Rebellion of 1641 began as a political rebellion led by the prominent O'Neill family of Ulster, who wanted to recover its property from Protestants and overthrow the Puritan government then holding Ireland. The O'Neills had ordered their followers not to hurt anyone, but there was no stopping the crowd once it was unleashed. What started out as a political protest turned into an all-out attack on Protestant farmers as the Catholic commoners let their resentment bubble over. That November, Irish Catholics killed thousands of Protestants. No one knows how many died; estimates range from 2,000 (as suggested by some historians) to 150,000 (as claimed by Protestant pamphle-teers). Many more lost their homes and property.

The attacks on Protestants by Catholics were bad, but they were nothing compared to the way they were described by English propa-gandists in London. They called it a "massacre." Pamphleteers inflated the Protestant death toll to nearly 150,000, and used extreme creativity in describing the horrors that the Catholics had inflicted upon them. The English public had always suspected that the Irish were barbaric, and this confirmed their suspicions. Now they were out for blood.

HOW DID OLIVER CROMWELL COME INTO POWER?

The 1641 rebellion coincided with a crisis in the English parliament that eventually turned to civil war. King Charles I was beheaded, and the leader who emerged from the crisis was one of the most puri-tanical Protestants in England—Oliver Cromwell. Cromwell had no problem believing that the Irish Catholics had committed any num-ber of atrocities, so he put together one of the most lethal armies in Europe to punish them.

The Irish leadership at that time was split between the Old Irish—led by Owen Roe O'Neill, Hugh O'Neill's nephew—and the Old English, led by the earl of Ormond from the Butler family. Although O'Neill and Ormond agreed that Ireland should remain Catholic, they opposed Cromwell for different reasons. O'Neill wanted Ireland to be independent, whereas Ormond opposed Cromwell because he saw him as a usurper against the real king, Charles II. This ideological difference made it difficult for them to work together and ultimately aided Cromwell's campaign of conquest.

HOW DID OLIVER CROMWELL CRUSH THE IRISH RESISTANCE?

It took Cromwell until 1649 to clear up things at home sufficiently to launch his Irish campaign, but, when he came, he meant business. Cromwell's army of 20,000 was efficient, well armed, and prepared for a bloody war. The army's initial engagements were marked by extreme savagery; Cromwell wanted revenge for the supposed Catholic butchery of 1641, and he wanted to terrify the rest of Ireland into surrendering.

Here were some of Cromwell's less admirable achievements:

* He destroyed Drogheda, massacred the population, sent the heads of the leaders to Dublin on poles, and sold the survivors to slave plantations in Barbados.
* Also in Drogheda, he burned down St. Peter's Church to abolish the people who sought asylum inside; he later called his acts "a righteous judgment of God upon these barbarous wretches."
* Again at Drogheda, he had his soldiers kill the garrison commander by beating out the man's brains with the commander's own wooden leg.
* He massacred the people of Wexford, including 300 women seeking clemency at the town cross.

- He had all the Catholic citizens of Cork expelled from their homes.
- At Bishop's Rock in Inishbofin, off the coast of Connemara, he tied a priest to a rock and forced his comrades to watch as the tide washed over him.

Cromwell aimed to terrify the population, and he certainly succeeded. By 1653 the Irish resistance was completely destroyed.

One of Cromwell's goals in Ireland was to break the power of the Catholic Church, and for a time he succeeded. While on campaign, he had Catholic priests hunted down and banished. Throughout the country he had churches desecrated and their sacred books and art destroyed. The priests who escaped his army had to disguise themselves in order to remain on the island. Although Irish Catholicism was by no means destroyed, it would take decades to recover.

IRISH PROVERB

If the knitter is weary, the baby will have no new bonnet.

Once English control was firmly established in 1653, Parliament passed an act to confiscate all Catholic-owned land in Ireland. Cromwell wanted to transplant all Catholics to the western province of Connacht so that he could settle his own soldiers and Protestant supporters on the more fertile land of Munster, Leinster, and Ulster. Although the eventual settlement didn't force all Catholics off their land, thousands of families were forced to leave their homes and resettle on the rocky terrain of Connacht.

HOW DID A BATTLE BETWEEN TWO BRITISH KINGS START THE PROTESTANT ASCENDANCY IN IRELAND?

A wave of excitement went through Ireland when James II rose to the English throne in 1685. James II was the first Catholic monarch in England since Mary, Queen of Scots. Former landowners who had lost their positions and property thought James would restore them to their former glory. James boosted these men's confidence when he appointed the earl of Tyrconnell, a Catholic, as his viceroy in Ireland.

To show James his support, Tyrconnell raised a Catholic army in Ireland. But this wasn't the sort of support that James needed just then. The king's religion had made his reign shaky from the start and an Irish-Catholic army was about the most alarming thing a good English Protestant could have imagined. Things went from shaky to really, really shaky, and in 1688 James fled to France.

Once James had run off, Parliament gave the crown to his Protestant daughter, Mary, and her husband, William of Orange. In Ireland, however, people still supported James II. James borrowed an army from France's Louis XIV, a fellow Catholic, and sailed to Kinsale Harbor in 1689. He joined up with Tyrconnell's Irish army and began to set up a power base from which he could regain the throne.

William, meanwhile, was skillfully working the European political scene and arrived in Ireland in 1690 with an international army of 36,000 soldiers. His forces swept through James's smaller Franco-Irish army at the Battle of the Boyne in July. James still had substantial resources that he could call up on his home territory, but he got spooked and fled to France again.

James's Catholic allies were left with the task of regrouping and facing William twelve months later at the Battle of Aughrim. This was another decisive victory for William.

The Irish army made its last stand at Limerick, but it had no chance of success. It sued for peace on the conditions that Catholics be spared religious persecution and that they have a guarantee of the same limited religious freedoms they'd had under Charles II. William agreed to the terms. William did not stick to the terms agreed to at Limerick, however.

As soon as he didn't need his European allies, he rolled back all his promises. A new round of confiscations robbed Catholics of their land, and a series of penal laws imposed harsh restrictions on the civil and economic rights of Catholics. This period of Irish history is known as the Protestant Ascendancy.

PART 7

The Protestant Ascendancy and the Roman Catholic Church

In the Middle Ages (c.500–c.1500 C.E.), just about everyone in Ireland was Catholic, as was nearly everyone in England, Scotland, and Wales. Catholic churches were everywhere, in every town. Most people were baptized after birth, attended Mass, married in a church, and were buried in church cemeteries. During the Protestant Ascendancy, however, the Anglican social elite dominated Ireland. They comprised only about 25 percent of the population, but they owned most of the property and controlled law, politics, and society. For Ireland's native Catholic majority, it was a time of poverty and oppression. What do you know about Ireland's religious conflict?

WHY WERE SOME PROTESTANT ARISTOCRATS ABSENTEE LANDLORDS?

The Treaty of Limerick of 1691 ended the violent wars that had ravaged Ireland in the seventeenth century. In the treaty, King William promised that Catholics would retain the right to practice their religion, and he gave the general impression that they would be treated fairly once they gave up their arms. Unfortunately, this proved not to be true. The king's true intention was to install a ruling class of Protestant landowners who would be loyal to the British Crown.

The victorious English government seized Catholic land to give to its Protestant supporters. The same thing had happened under the reigns of Elizabeth I, James I, and Cromwell. This time, however, the English were playing for keeps.

Members of the Protestant upper class had mixed feelings about their new home and their place in it. Aristocrats who had moved from England felt as if they were living on a frontier, almost like colonists in the New World or in Africa. Some of them definitely didn't like Ireland and spent as little time there as possible; these were known as absentee landlords, who lived off the proceeds of Irish land and labor but contributed nothing themselves.

WHY DID THE PENAL LAWS BAN IRISH CULTURE AND MUSIC?

The now-Protestant parliament enacted a series of infamous penal laws designed to limit Catholic power by curtailing Catholics' economic and social rights. Catholics were not allowed to bear arms, send their children to other countries for school, acquire land from Protestants, or make wills. Instead of deciding for themselves how their children would inherit, Catholics had to divide their property equally among all their sons, which resulted in increasingly small farms. There was an insidious catch, however—if the oldest son converted to the Protestant Church of Ireland, he inherited everything.

Irish clergy were expelled from the country. The Irish were not allowed to maintain schools, and in 1728 they lost the right to vote. All Irish culture and music was banned.

The penal laws didn't outlaw Catholicism, but they did make life very difficult for Catholics. The purpose of the laws was to keep Catholics from achieving enough wealth or legal power to challenge their Protestant rulers, and in that they were successful. It took more than 100 years before Catholics were able to mount any serious opposition to their subjugated state.

The penal laws didn't just hit Catholics. Ulster was home to a number of Scottish Presbyterians (the Scots-Irish) who also refused to accept the strictures of the Church of Ireland, and they too lost a good deal of political power. When push came to shove, though, the Ulster Presbyterians generally joined forces with their fellow Protestants against the Catholics.

WHY DID CATHOLICS PRAY AT MASS STONES?

In response to the penal laws, a few of the educated folks converted to Protestantism and kept their jobs and property. Most Catholics, though, were forced to give up their lands and their careers and move. Thousands ended up in the south and west of Ireland, especially in rocky Connacht.

The Protestants took over most of the existing large churches, but that didn't prevent Catholics from hearing Mass. Priests performed Mass out in the open countryside on large, flat stones called Mass stones. The people posted lookouts to spot approaching armies and warned the participants in time for them to escape. This could be a dangerous business; tales from this period tell of the English hunting priests for sport or of ex-priests turning in their former colleagues to collect bounties.

As the 1700s wore on, the Protestants relaxed their enforcement of the penal laws. A Catholic middle class began to appear as Irish Catholics, forbidden from owning land, poured their energies into trade. Some of them were quite successful. As this happened, Protestants began to identify more with Catholics; they still didn't want to grant them equal rights, but they were united by their resentment of the British government.

Nevertheless, the penal laws remained on the books. Protestants were only too aware that their property had originally been in Catholic hands, and they wanted to keep the laws even if they weren't often enforced. Irish Protestants were particularly worried that the British parliament might one day cave in to Catholic pressure and change laws to Protestant disadvantage.

WHAT IRISH CITY BECAME A CENTER OF ART AND HIGHER EDUCATION DURING THE ASCENDANCY?

The city of Dublin flourished during the Ascendancy. Aristocrats built themselves grand houses in the Georgian style. Urban planners designed a system of bridges and roads that allowed Dublin to expand into a city that stunned visitors from other countries who didn't expect to find urban grandeur in Ireland.

The stability of the 1700s allowed professional and intellectual societies to develop and the arts to flourish. The Dublin Society was founded in 1731 to encourage the arts, manufacturing, and agriculture. Its members helped develop a distinctively Irish style of architecture and sponsored many large projects, such as botanical gardens and drawing schools. The Royal Irish Academy, founded in 1785, encouraged the study of Irish culture and history.

Many of Ireland's most beautiful country estates, gardens, and urban architecture date to the Protestant Ascendancy period. One impressive estate is Powerscourt House in Enniskerry, near Dublin (its famous gardens weren't built until the nineteenth century, however). Phoenix Park, opened in 1747, is one of the largest city parks in the world—more than twice as big as New York's Central Park. The Custom House, built in the 1780s, was the first major project of the famous architect James Gandon. He followed this project with designs for the Four Courts, consisting of the High Court and Supreme Court of Ireland. Gandon also had a hand in renovating the cupola of the spectacular Rotunda Hospital, opened in 1757 as Europe's first maternity hospital.

WHY DID ELIZABETH I FOUND TRINITY COLLEGE?

Trinity College came into its prime in the 1700s. Queen Elizabeth I founded it in 1592 to provide an institute of higher education for Protestants in Ireland; for most of its history, it was completely Protestant. Catholics were admitted in 1793, but it wasn't until 1970 that Catholics could enroll without being excommunicated from the Catholic Church; the majority of its current students are Catholic.

Many of the college's most important buildings were designed and built in the 1700s, including the Old Library, which now houses the *Book of Kells*. Trinity College was open to a variety of social classes. Though everyone who went there was Anglican (and male), they were certainly not all noblemen. Many famous Irishmen of this period got their start there.

WHAT IS PROTESTANT IRISH NATIONALISM?

Once the Protestants had the Catholics under control, they started to examine their own situation vis-à-vis a larger power. Given that Ireland had its own parliament, the Anglo-Irish questioned why the British parliament had the right to pass legislation for Ireland.

IRISH BLESSING

May those who love us love us.

And those that don't love us,

May God turn their hearts.

And if He doesn't turn their hearts,

May he turn their ankles,

So we'll know them by their limping!

The Protestants in Ireland began to see the Emerald Isle as their home, and they wanted it to be a nation distinct from Britain. Economics were a big concern; the British government regularly obstructed Irish economic development by restricting Irish trade. As Irish businessmen expanded their operations, they wanted to export their products, and British law often didn't allow that. Consequently, the Irish Protestants began to take a keener interest in the political process. This was the start of Protestant Irish Nationalism; its proponents became known as "patriots."

Now, the Irish parliament, which the Normans brought to Ireland in the 1100s, was no paragon of democratic virtue. In the early eighteenth century, it consisted solely of members of the established Church of Ireland. The House of Lords was full of conservative bishops, and the House of Commons was composed of local clergy sent to Parliament on behalf of their wealthy patrons. Most of these men were more interested in feathering their own nests than in tackling constitutional issues, but at least they constituted a modicum of representational government independent of Britain.

HOW DID AMERICA'S REVOLUTIONARY WAR BRING PROTESTANTS AND CATHOLICS TOGETHER?

The American War of Independence was bad news for British rule in Ireland. The Irish, both Catholic and Protestant, saw Britain's treatment of Ireland as analogous to its treatment of the American colonies, and they observed the American Revolution with keen interest. The American Declaration of Independence was greeted in Ireland with glee. The British responded by cracking down further on Ireland, trying to limit its trade with America.

In 1779, Henry Grattan, a young Irish Protestant, made a motion in Parliament to abolish the British restriction on Irish exports. He won this argument and proceeded to lead the Irish parliament until the end of the century; the Parliament of this period is known as Grattan's Parliament.

Many Irish people, both Protestant and Catholic, were fully behind the Nationalist patriots. In the late 1770s, groups of Protestant men, known as Volunteers, joined the Irish cause—by 1779 there were Volunteers all over Ireland. Their main goals were to secure Irish free trade and to fight English interference with Irish government.

Grattan and other leaders realized they couldn't achieve independence from Britain without the help of the Catholic majority. So in 1778, Grattan pushed a Catholic Relief Act through Parliament; this act repealed some of the prohibitions on Catholic property ownership and inheritance. Grattan continued to rally his supporters and in 1779 won free trade rights for Ireland.

Pleased with his success, Grattan drafted an Irish declaration of independence in 1780. This measure passed in 1782 and gave Ireland the right to govern itself through its Parliament and judiciary. England still sent a viceroy to Dublin, and Dublin Castle was still answerable to the Crown, but it seemed to be a step forward.

The French Revolution, which began in 1789, gave more encouragement to Irish patriots. The Ulster Presbyterians were especially excited by the execution of Louis XVI and Marie Antoinette and the declaration of a French Republic. France seemed to be a model of religious tolerance, and the more idealistic Irish Protestant leaders accordingly decided that equality for Catholics would be good, or at least helpful to their cause.

HOW DID THE SOCIETY OF UNITED IRISHMEN USE THE POOR TO HELP ITS CAUSE?

In 1791 in Belfast, a young Protestant named Theobald Wolfe Tone founded the Society of United Irishmen. The United Irishmen's goal was to unite Irish people of all religions, to emancipate Catholics politically, to end the dominance of landlords, and to achieve political independence for Ireland. Wolfe Tone became secretary of the Catholic Association in Dublin, and through his efforts the Catholic population regained a number of the rights they had lost a century earlier. Catholic Relief Acts in 1792 restored the right to education, to practice law, to vote in local and parliamentary elections, and to bear arms. Catholics still couldn't sit in Parliament.

England didn't sit idle while this was going on. It formed a militia of citizens and passed the Convention Act to prevent public assemblies. In 1794 the British government repressed the United Irishmen in Dublin. The result was that the Irish people met in secret, and more of them began to agitate for more extreme reforms.

Wolfe Tone decided that the key to success was attracting the poor to his movement, and he emphasized with the United Irishmen's commitment to protecting Catholics. Catholics were ready for action, and many joined his cause. But other Protestants weren't sure they wanted to align themselves with Catholics. This tension was especially bad in the north, where Catholics had flocked in the wake of the new free-trade laws. Local Protestants feared Catholic competition in the profitable linen industry, and had been raised to fear Catholic theology as the teachings of the devil. The growing population didn't help, either, especially because Protestants saw Catholics as producing far more children than they did.

This tension found an outlet in secret agrarian societies, such as the Whiteboys and the Ribbonmen, which Catholics joined to protest unjust taxes or other points of contention; Protestants had their own groups. In South Ulster, the tension turned into a clear-cut conflict between Catholics and Protestants. Protestants in that area formed an armed group called the Peep O'Day Boys, and the Catholics responded with a group called the Defenders. These groups fought often; their most bloody battle was the 1795 Battle of the Diamond, in which the Protestants trounced the Catholics.

The victorious Protestants set up an organization called the Orange Order to protect their supremacy; they called themselves Orangemen. Many were government officials and leaders of the established church. The Catholics felt that the government was siding with the Orangemen and failing to protect them from Orange atrocities. This increasingly drove Catholics to side with Wolfe Tone and the United Irishmen, who were explicitly open to all religions and actively courted Catholic support.

WHY DID THEOBALD WOLFE TONE COMMIT SUICIDE?

In the second half of the 1790s, Wolfe Tone planned an armed rebellion against the English. He got to work drumming up military assistance for this enterprise, traveling to America and to France to rouse support for the Irish cause. His first efforts met with little success. In December 1796, he tried to land in Ireland with a group of French soldiers, but bad weather prevented his landing.

The British government increased its repression of the United Irishmen. It had a network of spies that kept the authorities in Dublin Castle well informed of Irish movements. Things came to a head in 1798. The United Irishmen had planned a huge rebellion in Dublin and had collected more than 20,000 pikes to use against British soldiers. Before they could get started, British troops marched into Dublin. They arrested the leaders of the Dublin United Irishmen and searched houses all over the city, turning up quite a pile of pikes.

Many Irish decided to go ahead with their rebellion and started small-scale efforts all over the country. They were poorly armed and disorganized without their leaders in Dublin, and the British quickly put them down. Between 30,000 and 50,000 Irish people rebelled, and many of them lost their lives. The French sent a small group of troops to Ireland to help the rebels, but they were quickly captured. Wolfe Tone was among them, dressed as a French officer. The British took him to Dublin and sentenced him to death, but he committed suicide in prison before he could be executed.

HOW DID THE IRISH PARLIAMENT VOTE ITSELF OUT OF EXISTENCE?

In 1800 the British parliament passed the Act of Union in both British and Irish parliaments, which created the "United Kingdom of Great Britain and Ireland." This act dissolved the Irish parliament and instead created seats for Irishmen in the British parliament in London. In passing this act, the Irish parliament essentially voted itself out of existence. The Act of Union polarized Protestant-Catholic relations by forcing Protestants to align themselves with Britain. It also paved the way for the career of one of the most important patriots in Irish history, the Liberator.

WHAT PATRIOT WAS KNOWN AS "THE LIBERATOR"?

Daniel O'Connell came from an aristocratic Catholic family in County Kerry. As a boy, he studied briefly at an informal hedge school, where he learned Gaelic history. He then went to school in France, where he observed the French Revolution firsthand; it's thought that the bloody events he witnessed there contributed to his avoidance of violence later in his political career. He was one of the first Irish Catholics to practice law after Catholics won back that right in the late 1700s.

O'Connell was strongly opposed to a union between Ireland and Britain. In 1823, he established the Catholic Association, a political organization whose goal was to force Britain's Parliament to admit Catholics. The association was open to all Catholics, rich or poor, and quickly became very popular. Even the poorest could afford the symbolic dues of one penny a month.

O'Connell was a brilliant orator, and his followers loved his style and his rhetoric, in which he claimed that the poor would soon inherit the Earth. He promised that if the Act of Union were repealed, the Irish would have rent security, unjust rents would be ended, votes would become secret, more people would be allowed to vote, and landlords would be taxed to support the poor.

In 1828, O'Connell himself ran for Parliament as a representative from County Clare and won. This presented a problem for the British because, since the days of Queen Elizabeth I, anyone taking public or church office was required to swear an Oath of Supremacy, which acknowledged the British monarch as the head of church and state. Anyone who refused to take the oath could be charged with treason.

Catholics who believed that the pope in Rome was the head of the Church obviously couldn't swear this oath, so it kept them out of office.

But O'Connell called the British bluff; he refused to take the Oath of Supremacy, and Parliament capitulated by allowing him into office without it. It did this by passing the Catholic Emancipation Act in 1829. This act allowed Catholics to enter Parliament and hold other important political offices without taking the oath. This accomplishment won O'Connell his famous nickname, the Liberator.

The Catholic Emancipation Act wasn't a perfect law; it mainly benefited the richer, middle-class Catholics. It actually made matters worse for the poor because it raised the rent requirement for voting to £10 a year. This disenfranchised most poorer property renters—now only about 1 percent of the Irish population could vote. It also took away any incentive landlords had to keep small tenants on their land and made the thought of using the land for profitable livestock more appealing. Landlords began getting rid of their tenants, which is one of the reasons the Great Famine was so devastating.

O'Connell's next goal was to get the Act of Union repealed, mainly so that the Irish parliament could be reinstated. His poorer Irish compatriots wanted faster action than he could provide working in the British parliament. They were disappointed that Catholic Emancipation hadn't been more profitable to them, and they began to take action for themselves.

O'Connell had kept agrarian secret societies, such as the Ribbonmen, quiet while he worked for emancipation, but now they rose up and again began to commit crimes against landlords. One continuing bone of contention was that Catholics had to pay tithes for the upkeep of Protestant clergy. In the 1830s, many Catholics refused to pay these tithes; this campaign became known as the Tithe War.

O'Connell kept working with the British Whig government to good effect. Through his efforts, Catholics won the right to be elected to important civic offices, and the Protestant Orange Order was quelled; the Orangemen didn't regain their strength until the 1880s. Tithes to the Church of Ireland were reduced, and some Poor Laws were passed to help the destitute. Most important for O'Connell, the Municipal Corporations Act of 1840 introduced more democratic local elections; as a result of this reform, O'Connell was elected mayor of Dublin.

These reforms were nice, but they didn't get to the root of Ireland's concerns—its continuing domination by the United Kingdom. In 1840, O'Connell founded the National Repeal Association, supported by the Catholic clergy and the Irish people. He declared 1843 "Repeal Year," and held "monster meetings"—huge and raucous gatherings—throughout Ireland to show the British government that he had ample support.

WHY DID DANIEL O'CONNELL GIVE IN TO THE BRITISH?

O'Connell's movement was undone by his insistence on nonviolence. The night before his last scheduled monster meeting, which was to have been held on the site of Brian Boru's famous victory at Clontarf, the British government made the gathering illegal. O'Connell acquiesced rather than allow fighting to erupt.

That was the end of his great influence in Irish politics. His followers had seen him as a messiah, but now they felt that he had surrendered to the British. Many of them also disagreed with his insistence
that Ireland was first and foremost a Catholic nation, arguing that
politics should come before religion. These young men founded a new
group, the Young Irelanders, which was to play an important political
role in the second half of the nineteenth century.

WHAT IS MODERN CATHOLICISM LIKE IN IRELAND?

The Catholic Church has remained powerful in Ireland throughout
the twentieth century. It played a major part in the emergence of the
Irish Free State and still dictates much of the structure of the Irish family. There are still Catholic churches everywhere in Ireland, and priests
in them say Mass regularly.

Ireland is more strongly tied to Rome than many other Catholic
countries in Europe. When Pope John Paul II visited Ireland in 1979,
people traveled for days and camped out overnight in the hope of getting a glimpse of him. Irish Catholicism also has an extraordinary number of links to its Celtic and medieval past. Some religious holidays have
direct links to pagan festivals; for example, the annual pilgrimage to
Croagh Patrick originated in the Celtic festival of Lughnasa.

For most of the twentieth century, the Church controlled state-
supported schools, which meant that almost all children were educated by priests, monks, and nuns. Some Irish remember the Catholic

schools of their youth fondly. Others recall brutal physical punishments and being afraid to tell their parents for fear that their parents would beat them, too, so strongly did they believe in the Church's authority.

The Church has been present in family life as well. Irish often have crosses or religious pictures of the pope, the Sacred Heart, or a favorite saint in their homes. Most Irish parents name their children after patron saints. Weddings and funerals almost invariably take place in a church; secular services are not popular. The Irish give more money to Catholic charities per capita than the people of any other European nation.

Up through the 1950s, many young Irish people chose religious vocations. Priests have long been honored and respected, and Irish priests have a reputation for being loving and devoted to their parishioners, though they can also be quite strict. Children and teenagers saw priests, monks, and nuns regularly, at church and at school, and the Church maintained a strong recruiting organization. Families who produced priests were praised, and many parents encouraged their children to seek a religious vocation. (Traditionally, it was a status symbol to have a priest or nun in the family, because it showed that the family had enough money to pay for religious education.)

The Church has played a very active role in modern Irish politics. The Irish Free State was set up in 1922 to be completely secular, but its leaders saw the Church as an Irish institution that distinguished them from the English. The Catholic archbishop Charles McQuaid of Dublin helped Éamon de Valera draft the constitution, which is explicitly Catholic. It guaranteed the Church a "special position" as the guardian of the faith of the majority of Irish citizens (the clause was removed in 1972).

PART 8

The Irish Potato Famine

An Gorta Mór, the Great Potato Famine of the 1840s, is one of the pivotal events in Irish history. Millions emigrated, and the resulting demographic shift led to a decreasing population. The famine also ignited anger at the British government, which eventually grew into the Irish independence movement. How could the simple spud cause so much trouble? Let's see how much you know!

WHAT CAUSED THE GREAT POTATO FAMINE?

Potatoes came to Europe from the New World in the early sixteenth century. Sir Francis Drake is thought to have introduced the potato to England, and shortly afterward Sir Walter Raleigh tried planting them on his Irish estates.

When potatoes reached Ireland, they created a revolution. They were very easy to grow; farmers could plant them in the spring and leave them alone for months while they went off and worked elsewhere (anywhere that scarce wages might be offered). People grew potatoes on any patch of land that could sustain them, even the most marginal of fields.

Potatoes are extremely nutritious; they are full of vitamins, protein, calcium, and iron, especially when washed down with buttermilk, the potato's traditional accompaniment. The potato, in fact, is perhaps the only crop that can provide a balanced diet by itself, which kept the Irish healthier than other people living on one starch such as rice or millet or even bread (made of wheat). It was relatively easy to store over the winter, which was important because most tenant farmers had no buildings in which to store vast quantities of grain. Unfortunately, you can't store potatoes for much more than a year, and this would have devastating consequences for the Irish in the famine years.

Patterns in land ownership made Irish farmers dependent on the potato. Most farmers had to rent from landlords (who were usually English) who demanded cash payments. The farmers had to use most of their time and land to produce cash crops to cover the rent, and consequently they only had small amounts of time or land left to grow their own food. Given these constraints, the potato was the only crop that could provide sufficient nutrition to feed the growing Irish families.

So there the Irish were, planting their potatoes every spring, digging them up every fall, and eating rather well, all things considered. But in the autumn of 1845, all that changed.

In October of that year, farmers walked out to their fields to harvest their crops. They plunged their shovels into the ground and then shrieked in horror—the potatoes were black and rotten, completely useless. The crop they had counted on for generations had finally failed them.

No one knew what to do. Experts offered advice, suggesting that the fungus killing the potatoes was attracted to moisture. Farmers tried to dig dry pits, but the spores traveled through the air and soaked into the ground after the rain, which has always been plentiful in Ireland. It took only one infected plant to spread the blight over acres of potatoes. There was no escape.

The worst part of the potato blight was that it didn't go away. After the 1845 crops failed, people counted on the potatoes of 1846 to pull them through, but those potatoes rotted away, too. For some reason the crop of 1847 survived, but not enough fields of potatoes had been planted to produce enough food for everyone who needed it. And in 1848 the blight reappeared with a vengeance.

WHAT HAPPENED DURING "THE BAD TIMES"?

The poor Irish who had lost their potatoes faced terrifying difficulties. They called the time *an Gorta Mór*, which means "the Great Hunger," or *an Drochshaol,* "the Bad Times." The poorest farmers, already living at a subsistence level, were the first to feel the effects. Within a few months of the bad harvest, the people in the hardest-hit areas were already dying of starvation. Travelers reported seeing skeletal people with their mouths stained green; they had tried to ward off hunger by eating grass. In some places in western Ireland, piles of corpses filled the ditches.

Typhus appeared in the winter of 1846. The Irish called it the "black fever" because it made victims' faces swollen and dark. It was incredibly contagious, spread by lice, which were everywhere. Many people lived in one-room cottages, humans and animals all huddled together, and there was no way to avoid lice jumping from person to person. The typhus bacteria also traveled in louse feces, which formed an invisible dust in the air. Anyone who touched an infected person, or even an infected person's clothes, could become the disease's next victim. Typhus was the supreme killer during the famine; in the winter of 1847, thousands of people died of it every week.

Another fever appeared at the same time, the relapsing fever called "yellow fever" because its victims became jaundiced. This fever was also carried by lice. A victim suffered from a high fever for several days, seemed to recover, and then relapsed a week later. Many people died from this fever as well.

Scurvy also became a problem. This disease comes from a deficiency of vitamin C, and it causes the victim's connective tissue to break down. The Irish called scurvy "black leg," because it made the blood vessels under the skin burst, giving a victim's limbs a black appearance. The cure for scurvy is fresh food—meat, vegetables, or fruit—none of which was available to the poor in Ireland.

There were other diseases, too. Some Irish children fell victim to an odd disease that made hair grow on their faces while it fell out of their heads. Some observers commented that the children looked like monkeys. Cholera was also always a problem in unsanitary, crowded conditions; it broke out in workhouses throughout the famine years.

HOW DID FAMINE VICTIMS DEAL WITH THE DEAD?

When people died, the living were left with the problem of what to do with the bodies. There were not enough coffins to hold the dead, even if the poor had had money to pay for them. Stories abounded of entire families dying, or of mothers losing all their children and carrying the bodies to the cemetery on their backs, one by one. Visitors reported seeing dead bodies stacked in ditches and dogs devouring corpses in the fields; to their horror, they also observed people killing and eating those same dogs.

When someone came down with typhus, relatives and neighbors feared they would contract the disease, too. Sometimes all healthy members of a family would leave a sick person alone in a house, hoping to escape the contagion. They hadn't abandoned the sufferer; they pushed food in through the windows on the end of a long pole. When there was no longer a response from inside the house, they pulled the house down on top of the victim and burned the whole thing.

HOW DID LANDOWNERS REACT TO THE CRISIS?

Most of the victims of the famine did not own the land they lived on. Instead, they rented houses and farmland from large landholders. When the potato crops failed, they could no longer pay their rents. Some landlords were understanding; many actually helped their tenants, handing out food and concocting jobs that would allow them to earn wages.

But other landlords were less accommodating. Scores of poor Irish were evicted from their homes. This wasn't all due to cruelty and greed; many landlords themselves faced bankruptcy and starvation as their rents stopped coming in. Some landlords decided that grazing sheep or cattle would be a better use of the land, and the peasants and their potato plots had to give way for the livestock.

The result was that many poor Irish found themselves not only starving, but homeless as well. Some of them moved into workhouses, but many dug holes in hillsides or made huts out of peat and lived in them as best they could. Others simply wandered the roads until they dropped dead.

WHO BLAMED OVERPOPULATION FOR THE FAMINE?

One of the things that made the Irish famine especially bad was a lack of help for the starving. The British government was reluctant to help too much, partly out of fear that the poor would depend on aid and not try to help themselves. The mid-nineteenth century was the heyday of laissez-faire economics, which taught that the free market would solve all problems and that the government should never intervene. Unfortunately, that approach led to tragedy for the Irish population.

Politicians quickly got word that the Irish peasantry had nothing to eat. Many English were not particularly impressed with the Irish plight. A number of them thought that the famine was a punishment for Ireland's sin of overpopulation. According to population theorist Thomas Robert Malthus, Ireland had far too many people for its land to support, and the best solution was to get rid of most of them. The famine would take care of that.

The truth was, the factors that contributed to the Irish famine were far more complex than mere overpopulation. There was plenty of food in Ireland. The island grew and exported more than 1 billion pounds of grain every year. Many Irish actually sold this food willingly so they would have the money to pay rent. Ireland also was not allowed to import rice or corn from the British colonies. This was the effect of the Corn Laws (the British call wheat "corn"; they call corn "maize"), which set artificially high prices for British grain and locked out cheaper imports until the entire British crop was sold. This was a problem for the Irish, who had no money.

Prime Minister Robert Peel initially took pity on the starving Irish, and, unbeknownst to his own government, ordered Indian corn from the Americas to be delivered to the island. This corn was only a last resort for the sufferers; it was difficult to grind and cook, not nearly as filling as potatoes, and it lacked vitamin C. It ran out quickly, too, and was not replaced.

Peel resigned in 1846, and for the next four years the man he appointed to oversee famine relief, Charles Edward Trevelyan, handled matters. Trevelyan didn't have a very high opinion of the Irish, and in fact only visited Ireland once; he thought distance helped him maintain objectivity. He was a firm believer in laissez faire and thought donated food actually exacerbated the problem by relieving the Irish of the obligation to feed themselves. Unfortunately, in some places, no one had either food or money, so feeding themselves was completely impossible. Irish crops continued to be exported, which led to great resentment on the part of the Irish people.

HOW DID WEARING PAUPERS' UNIFORMS SAVE SOME PEOPLE FROM STARVING?

When people got truly desperate, there was a place they could go: the workhouse. These houses had been established in the early 1840s to provide relief to the poorest people. Opponents of workhouses feared that the Irish would abuse the system, using the workhouse even if they weren't truly desperate. But supporters countered that they could solve this problem by making workhouses so unpleasant that only people with no alternative would enter them.

Unpleasant they were. Anyone who owned land had to give it up before entering a workhouse, which forced many families to choose between staying on their farms and starving or giving up their land for a chance to eat. People who entered a workhouse were segregated by sex, which meant dividing up families. They were forced to live there, essentially sentencing themselves to prison. They had to give up their own clothes and wear pauper's uniforms, which marked them as destitute. They had to work at menial jobs to earn their keep—men broke up rocks, women knitted, and children either had lessons or learned to do various industrial tasks. Families only got together on Sundays.

The Irish people did everything they could to avoid the workhouse. They found the splitting up of families especially hard to bear. The unpleasant regimen did succeed in keeping people away from public charity in the early 1840s and even into 1846, before the second bad potato crop.

But after the second nonexistent potato harvest in the autumn of 1846, people were more willing to surrender their dignity in the hopes of not starving. Poorhouse food was bad and often inadequate, but at least it was food. By mid-October, most workhouses in the worst-hit areas were full and turning away inmates.

Crowding did nothing to improve the workhouse atmosphere. The stench became overpowering as hundreds of unhealthy people contributed their bodily products to the building. Typhus, cholera, and other diseases thrived in this environment, and many people died.

WHY WAS 1847 KNOWN AS BLACK '47?

Not everyone could fit into the workhouses, and many people refused to even consider the possibility. The government provided an alternative for them: working for pay on public projects. Local relief committees made lists of people who needed help, and then one member of each needy family was allowed to work for pay.

This was a nice idea, but ineffective in practice. The projects in question involved hard physical labor—digging ditches, breaking and moving rocks to build roads—and the workers were already malnourished. The winter of 1846–47 was especially harsh, and the workers had no adequate clothes. Many of them fell sick and dropped dead on the job. In fact, 1847 was such a bad year that it became known as Black '47.

A ROAD TO NOWHERE

Old famine roads from these make-work projects are still visible in western Ireland, where many of them have been converted to hiking trails or highways. The Dingle Peninsula contains a number of these roads and famine fences. Some roads travel by prehistoric tombs and other ancient Irish artifacts.

The wages for public works would have been generous in the days of plentiful potatoes, but during the famine food prices went through the roof. A week's wages were barely adequate to buy half a week's sustenance for a family of any size, and many Irish families were large. Families were desperate to keep someone on the works to collect money, though, so they often deprived nonworkers of food to keep up the strength of the wage earners. Children went hungry so their fathers could eat.

In many cases, the person going out to work was also the person who would have planted the next year's potato crop at home. Without that labor, the next year's harvest suffered.

HOW DID THE GOVERNMENT MAKE THE CRISIS WORSE?

In 1847, the government stopped the public-works programs and announced that from now on, private aid would be the solution. The British still feared that too much aid to the Irish would prevent them from ever going back to work. The British decided that Irish landlords must be responsible for the famine, so it would be their job to fix it. Local governments were supposed to organize charitable soup kitchens paid for by taxes collected by local relief committees.

But as the famine years progressed, Ireland had less and less food and money. Landlords went bankrupt as their tenants failed to pay rents, and property taxes went up, ironically, to provide money to feed the starving. In an effort to lower their property values and thus their taxes, some of them evicted the peasants still living on their land and tore down their huts. Britain sent more and more soldiers to Ireland to enforce evictions and see that taxes were collected. This combination of military might and no food made the Irish even more resentful of the occupying British government. Though there was more food available now, no one had the money to buy it.

IRISH PROVERB

If you lie down with dogs, you'll rise with fleas.

Matters were made even worse by a financial crisis in Britain in 1847. Wheat prices plummeted, railroad stocks fell, and many businesses went bankrupt. The British had less money to help the Irish, even if they had wanted to.

The winter of 1848–49 was a nightmare for the Irish. They had gambled on the potato crop, spending every cent they had to buy seed potatoes that they planted in the spring; after all, the blight hadn't attacked the 1847 crop, so they had reason to hope that it was gone. But they were terribly wrong; the blight was still around and it dev-astated potatoes all over the island. Landlords kept evicting peasants, and the British government kept raising Ireland's taxes in the vain hope that this would help the island pull itself up by its bootstraps. The poorest people shrank down to human skeletons before dying. Some turned to crime as an alternative to starvation—in prison or on a ship heading to Australia, they would at least have something to eat. Wealthier people gave up on Ireland and left for other countries.

HOW DID THE FAMINE CHANGE IRELAND PERMANENTLY?

Ireland was a different place after the famine. The population was dras-tically reduced—an island of 8.2 million people in 1841 was reduced to 6 million by 1851. At least 1 million of those people had died. The rest fled the country, hoping for a new life in another land.

After the famine, there were fewer tiny landholdings, farms of five or fewer acres. By 1851, many more farms consisted of thirty acres or more. Fathers stopped dividing their acreage among all their sons and instead passed the entire farm to just one of them. This made it easier for a farmer to support his own family but caused problems for the children who didn't inherit. It also forced inheriting sons to wait longer to come into property, which delayed marriages. Farmers used more of their land to grow livestock; not surprisingly, they didn't grow nearly as many potatoes as they had before.

Many Irish left their beloved homeland during the famine years, hoping to find something better in the United States, England, Canada, or Australia. Emigration posed its own risks. Many emigrants died en route to their destinations. Others found that their new homes were little better than the barren farms they'd left behind. Nevertheless, many Irish emigrants quickly grew roots in fresh soil and flourished. For better or for worse, the Irish were now permanently planted around the world.

In addition, the famine did a lot to foster a feeling of unity among the Irish against the English. Dedication to the Catholic Church increased and priests grew more powerful. The Irish especially hated the landlord-tenant system, which had forced so many of them out of their homes. People across the country formed societies to protect tenants by fixing rents and getting farmers to promise not to take over the lands of evicted tenants. Irish politicians began pushing the tenant agenda in Parliament, and their efforts formed the start of Ireland's independence movement.

On St. Patrick's Day, 1858, a former Young Ireland (a group of young men who fought for Irish independence) leader named James Stephens founded the Irish Republican Brotherhood. Around the same time, another rebel named Jeremiah O'Donovan Rossa founded a similar Phoenix Society in Skibbereen, County Cork. These movements spread rapidly during the late 1850s. Though they were strongly condemned by the Catholic Church, these independence movements continued to gather steam and plan insurrections that would lead to an Irish republic.

PART 9

Independence and Irish Nationalism

The Ireland that dragged itself out of the Great Hunger was changed forever. Lingering resentment began to take shape, leading to an organized political movement for independence. Eventually, the forces of Irish Nationalism won their independence, but the violent path they chose has left scars to this day. What do you know about Home Rule and Irish Nationalism?

WHAT IS THE IRISH
NATIONALIST MOVEMENT?

The Irish Nationalist Movement rose out of the anger people felt about the famine and the continuing economic disparities of their island. It first manifested itself in agrarian secret societies—groups of farmers and laborers who secretly gathered in the countryside to enforce their own views of justice, usually against landowners and their agents. Groups like this had existed for over a century, but in the 1850s their campaigns of rural terrorism and economic sanctions became more aggressive and targeted specifically the English. The most powerful of these secret societies was the Irish Republican Brotherhood (IRB), known commonly as the Fenians.

WHAT'S IN A NAME?

The name "Fenian" referred to Finn MacCool's legendary band of warriors, the Fianna, who defended Ireland in the distant past.

The principal mover behind the Fenians was James Stephens, a fiery orator with a gift for organization and a vague notion of an independent Irish nation. John O'Mahoney, the head of the powerful U.S. Fenian chapter, was his ally. Stephens and O'Mahoney built the Fenian Brotherhood into a secret, semirevolutionary society with thousands of members. They founded the newspaper *Irish People* to express their desire for land reform and Irish independence.

WHO ARE THE MANCHESTER MARTYRS?

In 1867 the Fenians took action. They didn't have enough weapons to pose any real threat to British military power, but they hoped that an act of armed defiance would encourage the people to rise up against England. They launched several raids to steal weapons from police and coast guard stations; unfortunately for them, the people did not rally to their aid as they had hoped, and most of their fighters got caught.

The English quickly broke up the Fenian military organization and imprisoned its leaders. They executed Fenian leaders William Allen, Michael Larkin, and Michael O'Brien on dubious legal grounds. These men became known as the Manchester Martyrs.

WHAT BRITISH PRIME MINISTER TRIED TO DEFUSE IRELAND'S HOME RULE PARTY?

After the famine, both Catholics and Protestants had begun to feel that the English could not rule their island effectively and justly. Although they had their own differences, an uneasy coalition of conservative Protestants and liberal Catholics got together and formed the Home Rule Party. This party got many of its members into Parliament at the same time that a liberal, Prime Minister William Gladstone, was emerging as a giant in British politics.

Gladstone realized that Ireland's complaints against England were justified and that England's presence in Ireland was based on a tradition of injustice; at the same time, he felt that the Home Rulers were too radical. He tried to defuse the Home Rule movement by enacting landmark legislation to address Irish grievances—killing Home Rule with kindness. His first act, in 1868, declared that the Protestant Church of Ireland was no longer the official religion of the entire country. Most Irish loved this. The act was cheered in Dublin but condemned in Belfast, where the population was mostly Protestant.

Gladstone's most important reforms were his Land Acts of 1870 and 1881. Before these acts, the average Irish farmer rented his farmland (usually from an English landowner) and lived in constant fear of eviction. The Land Acts granted these farmers protection against unreasonable rents and unfair evictions, and made it easier for them to buy land. Over time, the Land Acts greatly improved the lives of many farmers, and Gladstone's strategy might well have defused the Home Rule movement, if not for the emergence of one of Ireland's most charismatic leaders—Charles Stewart Parnell.

HOW WAS CHARLES STEWART PARNELL A LEADER IN LAND REFORM?

Parnell was handsome, impassioned, and articulate, and he took Parliament by storm. People didn't know what to make of him. He was a wealthy Protestant landowner, but at the same time he supported the radical Nationalist politics of poor Catholic farmers. He entered Parliament in 1875 as the representative for County Meath. His confident oratory and uncompromising dedication to land reform instantly made him a leader of the Home Rule Party. When he felt that Irish issues were being ignored in Parliament, he recruited his fellow Irish MPs to obstruct parliamentary proceedings until his issues were heard.

Parnell was president of the Land League, a farmers' organization that called for relief of exorbitant rents, more lenient eviction policies, and easier land ownership for small farmers. Gladstone's Land Acts had made some progress on these fronts, but that progress was too slow for Parnell. His Land League insisted that farmers evicted from their property should hold their ground, and it tacitly condoned the use of boycotts and violence against landlords who took possession of an evicted tenant's land. This period of rural intimidation and economic sanction became known as the Land War.

Gladstone didn't approve of Parnell's obstructionist policies and endorsement of Land League violence; he had Parnell arrested and thrown in Kilmainham Jail in 1881. Parnell continued to run his political machine from jail, and he achieved unprecedented popularity in Ireland for defying the prime minister.

Both Parnell and Gladstone, however, realized they needed to work together to achieve real reform. They carried on secret negotiations through two intermediaries, Captain Willie O'Shea and his wife, Katherine (Kitty). Gladstone and Parnell eventually reached a settlement called the Kilmainham Treaty, in which Parnell restrained Land League violence in exchange for his release and Gladstone's cooperation on a more powerful Land Act.

In the 1885 election, Parnell's Home Rulers took 85 of the 103 Irish seats in Parliament. It appeared that some form of constitutional solution to Home Rule was in sight. In 1886 Parnell and Gladstone brought forth a Home Rule Bill to finally give Ireland a form of independence.

There was a big problem, though—the Protestants in the northern part of Ireland (Ulster) didn't want Home Rule. The rise of the Home Rule Party called attention for the first time to a phenomenon that Irish Nationalists had traditionally ignored and would continue to ignore to their detriment—the loyalty of Ulster Unionists (those who wanted Ireland to remain part of the United Kingdom). That's why Protestants had founded the Orange Order during the time of Wolfe Tone. That's also why they created the militant Ulster Defence Association after Gladstone disestablished the Protestant Church in Ireland in 1868.

The 1886 Home Rule Bill didn't pass; it had too much opposition from Ulster and the British House of Lords, who still liked the idea of Ireland as part of the British Empire. Parnell regathered his forces and prepared to try again, but personal affairs suddenly intruded—Willie O'Shea divorced his wife, Kitty, and named Parnell as her lover. It was a huge scandal. Remember, the O'Sheas had served as Parnell's intermediaries for the Kilmainham Treaty. The trial revealed that Parnell and Kitty had been carrying on a passionate affair since then. Captain O'Shea had known about the affair for years; Kitty had already had three children with Parnell.

The case shocked both liberal Englishmen and Catholic Irishmen. Gladstone ended his alliance with Parnell, fearing that his own party in England wouldn't support him if he stuck with the Irishman. Parnell fell from power.

Parnell didn't give up. He married Kitty O'Shea and began a fierce campaign to retake his position in the party. His charisma and political skill were such that he might have actually succeeded, but a fever killed him suddenly in 1891. Kitty was beside him when he died. With Parnell's death, the Home Rule movement lost its momentum, and it didn't truly regain it for another twenty-five years.

WHAT WAS SINN FÉIN?

Although the independence movement had entered a period of contented inaction, radical Nationalism hadn't disappeared. The IRB (the group that organized the Fenian uprising) was still around, but its call for armed revolt seemed more and more like the talk of cranky old men.

The movement for an independent republic took a quiet step forward in 1905 when a publisher named Arthur Griffith founded a new political party called Sinn Féin, Irish for "ourselves alone." Griffith promoted the Nationalist cause in a newspaper called the *United Irishman*, after Wolfe Tone's old organization. Sinn Féin was a relatively small party throughout the prewar years, but it provided radicals and intellectuals with a place to discuss aggressive alternatives to the slow constitutional path to Home Rule.

How did the Ulster Protestants derail Home Rule?

Home Rule didn't make any progress in the Conservative-controlled Parliament during the first decade of the twentieth century. But when the Liberals swept back into power in 1910 behind Prime Minister Herbert Henry Asquith, Ireland was at the top of their agenda. In 1912, Asquith brought forward the third Home Rule Bill, which reached further than any of its predecessors and enjoyed wide popularity among the Irish people.

One section of the Irish population, however, still opposed Home Rule—the Ulster Protestants. Seeing the latest Home Rule Bill as the final step toward separation, the members of the Orange Order rose up against it. They organized the Ulster Volunteer Force (UVF), a paramilitary group committed to defending Ulster's union with England. The UVF began drilling and stockpiling weapons. By 1914 an estimated 100,000-plus men stood ready to fight for the UVF.

In response, Nationalists in the south began their own paramilitary organization called the Irish Volunteers. The Volunteers was initially organized by the remnants of the IRB, although its politics was generally closer to the moderates of the Home Rule Party. The Volunteers claimed to have more than 100,000 members as well, though it had fewer weapons than its rivals in the north.

The Ulster dilemma froze the Home Rule Bill in its tracks. Although the Liberals may have had sufficient votes to push the bill through, it was politically very awkward to push away a big group of loyal British subjects, especially when those subjects were threatening to fight to stay in. A favored solution to this problem was to grant Home Rule and then use the British army to enforce it in Ulster. This proposal faltered when the mutiny at the Curragh revealed that British army officers were opposed to fighting Ulster troops.

The second set of options revolved around some form of partition, in effect dividing Ireland into two states. There were nine counties in the traditional province of Ulster, but only six of them had large Protestant populations, and in 1910 only four of them had Protestant majorities. Unionists and Nationalists suggested different partition plans. Some supported having all of Ulster split off and stay with the United Kingdom, which might have facilitated reunification in the future. Others thought it would be better if only those counties with Protestant majorities broke away from the Irish nation. Both sides spent the next four years wrangling over various proposals, but none met the approval of both the Unionist and the Nationalist sides.

HOW DID WORLD WAR I LEAD TO UNREST IN IRELAND?

In August 1914, outside events suddenly changed the whole debate. World War I was breaking out in Europe, and Parliament wanted to solve the Irish problem quickly so that it could concentrate on the coming war. John Redmond, the leader of the Home Rulers, offered the United Kingdom the use of the Irish Volunteers for home defense in exchange for a provisional acceptance of the Home Rule Bill, leaving aside the Ulster question for the time being. Asquith's Parliament agreed, and the bill was put on the books with the proviso that it would not go into effect until a year had passed or the war was over. Both sides saw this as a way to move forward on the Ireland issue without coming to a final decision on Ulster.

The act was immediately received as a tremendous step forward for Ireland, and Nationalists felt free for the first time in decades to express British patriotism. Thousands of young men from all parts of Ireland came forward to serve in the war, including many members of the UVF and the Irish Volunteers. In the early days, morale was high.

As the war ground on, however, Irish opinions began to turn. Not only did the war delay the enactment of Home Rule, but each month brought new lists of Irish casualties from the battlefields of Europe as well. The British military didn't accept Redmond's offer to use the Volunteers, nor did it arm them for home defense. It was rumored that the English draft would soon spread to Ireland. To make matters worse, a change in government put Ulster Unionist leaders in the British Cabinet, making Nationalists suspect that Home Rule might be delayed indefinitely. It was in this environment that the radicals in the IRB and Sinn Féin decided to make their move.

WHAT WAS THE EASTER REBELLION?

On April 24, 1916, Easter Monday, a group of armed Irish Volunteers moved into the General Post Office in Dublin and occupied the building. Patrick Pearse (or Pádraig MacPiarais), a schoolteacher and Sinn Féin activist, read the Proclamation of the Irish Republic, a statement declaring Ireland's independence. Simultaneously, armed Volunteers took over other significant buildings throughout the city.

GOING POSTAL?

The General Post Office on O'Connell Street is one of Dublin's most famous landmarks. Today it is both a monument and a working post office. You can still see bullet holes in the wall, left there from the Easter Rebellion.

The uprising was a surprise for Unionists and Nationalists alike; with Home Rule already on the books, armed revolution seemed a little extreme. British troops were quickly sent into the city, and soon much of central Dublin was in flames. The Volunteers lacked either the arms or the organization to put up a real military resistance to the British army, and after a week the last of the rebels surrendered. The fighting killed 450, and afterward more than 1,000 Irish were sent to prisons in England.

At the time of the Easter Rebellion, most Irish people—even Nationalists—didn't think violence was the answer to Ireland's problems. Ensuing events, however, soon led to a change in opinions. In

May of 1916, the British army began executing leaders of the rebellion. They shot or hanged sixteen men. Most Irish thought the British had decided to execute the prisoners much too hastily and without fair trials. In addition, there were reports of imprisoned rebels being treated badly. The British released the remaining prisoners by Christmas 1916, primarily as a gesture to help bring the United States into the war, but that did little to quiet emotions in Ireland.

HOW DID SINN FÉIN FIGHT FOR A UNITED REPUBLIC OF IRELAND?

Prime Minister Asquith appointed David Lloyd George (who would replace Asquith as prime minister later that year) to resolve the Irish Home Rule question once and for all. Lloyd George, relying heavily on the advice of Unionist associates, settled on a compromise in which Ireland got Home Rule but the six majority Protestant counties in the north remained part of the Union (the British Empire).

To southern Nationalists, this was unacceptable. To make matters worse, the British army seized the weapons from Irish Volunteer groups in the south but allowed UVF forces to keep theirs. People in the south began to believe that the Home Rule Bill on the books was a charade.

This gave Sinn Féin its big chance. Led by Éamon de Valera, an American-born mathematician who had taken part in the Easter Rebellion, Sinn Féin began to take Parliament seats away from the traditional Home Rule candidates. Sinn Féin's stated goal was an independent, unified Republic of Ireland.

Sinn Féin's parliamentary successes were limited to Nationalist hotbeds until the British government gave them two great boosts: first, it extended army conscription to Ireland, an act the Irish had dreaded for years; second, it arrested de Valera and other Sinn Féin leaders on vague and insubstantial charges of a plot against the government. Both actions were highly unpopular, and they convinced the majority of the Irish that the British government was not serious about letting Ireland run its own affairs.

WHO WAS ÉAMON DE VALERA?

Éamon de Valera dominated twentieth-century Irish politics. He led Sinn Féin (1917–1926), the Irish provisional government (1919–1922), the anti-treaty forces (1922–1925), and then Fianna Fáil (1925–1975). He served for sixteen years as *taoiseach* (prime minister) and nineteen years as president. He retired from politics at the age of ninety-one and died two years later, in 1975. Throughout, de Valera was known as a fervent patriot, a devout Catholic, and an incorruptible servant of his people.

De Valera was born in New York in 1882 to an Irish mother and a Spanish father—hence his unusual name. This made him an American, which he used to his advantage throughout his political career. When he was three, his father died and his mother sent him to Ireland to be raised by his grandmother in Bruree, County Limerick. He studied mathematics in Dublin and became a teacher. He also came to love the Irish language and became involved with the Gaelic League, which led to his extreme Nationalism.

De Valera was an intellectual and he looked the part—tall, thin, and bespectacled. He didn't stand out from the crowd until he ended up in prison after the Easter Rebellion. Subsequently, his eloquent letters and well-thought-out arguments for Irish independence began to inspire a generation of young men, and they soon chose him as their leader.

WHO STARTED THE IRISH REPUBLICAN ARMY?

While Sinn Féin was taking the road of politics, a twenty-seven-year-old Easter Rebellion veteran named Michael Collins was exploring an alternate path. Working with the IRB and the Irish Volunteers, he began organizing a paramilitary force that could put guns behind Sinn Féin's claims of independence. This force became known as the Irish Republican Army—the IRA.

Michael Collins (1890–1922) played several extraordinary roles for the Nationalists: spymaster, guerrilla leader, minister of finance, diplomat, and, finally, tragic martyr. His exploits were legendary. Liam Neeson portrayed his life in the unabashedly patriotic movie *Michael Collins* (1996).

WHO WERE THE BLACK AND TANS?

Most Irish people deplored the IRA killings. Collins calculated that his systematic terrorism would provoke the English into an overly aggressive response. And that's exactly what happened.

The British shipped thousands of soldiers to Ireland and created a new police force called the Black and Tans to help keep the peace. The Black and Tans were composed primarily of former British soldiers who had neither the police training nor the familiarity with Ireland that the sensitive situation demanded. These men found Ireland very stressful— the people who murdered their fellow officers were indistinguishable from the people they were supposed to protect. So they responded with a campaign of reprisals that matched the IRA's in brutality.

This period of guerrilla strikes and police reprisals is known as the Anglo-Irish War. Both sides lost hundreds of men. The IRA made little military headway, but the war's impact on the opinions of the Irish people was devastating to the British. The peacekeeping strategy backfired. The Black and Tans' brutal and often indiscriminate reprisals convinced people that Sinn Féin was right after all and that Great Britain was a repressive occupier that would only relinquish Ireland if forced out.

HOW DID A PEACE TREATY
START THE IRISH CIVIL WAR?

The Anglo-Irish War was simultaneously playing havoc with British politics. English civilians were shocked by the daily stories of police brutality in Ireland. In composing the Treaty of Versailles at the end of the war, Britain claimed that World War I had been fought to protect the rights of small countries to determine their own fates, and yet it had a small country in its own backyard demanding its own rights—rights England was not willing to grant.

Prime Minister Lloyd George called for a cease-fire and treaty negotiations. The fact that he was offering a treaty was significant; only sovereign nations can sign treaties with one another, so his offer made it clear that independence was on the table. The Sinn Féin and IRA leaders agreed to the cease-fire, and a group of ambassadors led by Arthur Griffith and Michael Collins went to London in 1921 to negotiate.

Both sides agreed that Ireland would take a dominion status similar to that enjoyed by Canada—independent, but still a part of the British Empire. The chief sticking points were whether the Irish would have to swear an oath to the king, and the final settlement of the Ulster question.

After skillful negotiation by a British team, including Lloyd George and Winston Churchill, the Irish contingent largely gave in on both points. The final Treaty of Peace between Great Britain and Ireland did not demand that Irish citizens swear allegiance to the king, but it did require them to recognize his dominion over Ireland. More significantly, the treaty established the six-county partition of Ulster pushed for by Unionists since 1914. This action, called Partition, created the political entity called Northern Ireland.

Collins signed the treaty, saying it was the best that Ireland could achieve under the current conditions. After a bitter struggle, it was passed by the Dáil (the new Irish parliament). Not everyone was happy, however; Éamon de Valera condemned the treaty, as did the majority of radical Nationalists in the IRA. These Nationalists said that they had fought for a united Ireland, and they wouldn't take one cut into pieces. And so the Irish Civil War (1921–1923) began.

WHY DID ÉAMON DE VALERA PUT A STOP TO THE IRISH CIVIL WAR?

Like all civil wars, the Irish Civil War was marked by bitterness and atrocity. Collins was forced to organize an official military response against the same IRA men he had fought beside for years. Hundreds died, and Collins himself was killed in an ambush. The antitreaty forces, however, did not have the support of the populace, and it was soon clear that they could not win. To stop the bloodshed, Éamon de Valera announced that it was time for Ireland to accept the treaty and move on.

Ireland had peace and independence at last, but not without a cost. The scars of the Civil War haunted Irish politics for decades. More significantly, the division between the Irish Free State in the south and Northern Ireland had become real and immovable. Unionists in Northern Ireland, appalled by the violence of the Anglo-Irish and Civil Wars, resolved more strongly than ever to remain part of the United Kingdom. This unnatural division between north and south has plagued people on both sides of the border to this day.

PART 10

The Republic of Ireland

When the Irish Civil War ended, Ireland had peace and independence at last. Over the next fifty years, the people of Ireland worked through the difficult questions regarding their relationship with the United Kingdom, the role of the Catholic Church in their government, and the thorny question of Northern Ireland. What do you know about the creation of the Republic of Ireland?

WHAT WAS THE
IRISH FREE STATE?

The Ireland that emerged from the Anglo-Irish Treaty in 1921 was known as the Irish Free State. In many ways, it had the independence that Irish Nationalists had dreamed about for years. It had its own Parliament, the Dáil Éireann (doyl AY-ran), which was responsible for Ireland's social and economic affairs. It inherited a British government infrastructure that allowed it to jump quickly into efficient self-government. Police and Irish home defense forces were now entirely under Ireland's control, with a new, unarmed police force known as the Garda Síochána (GAR-dah sho-HA-na).

But the Free State still maintained a number of ties to England. It was still subject to British international policy, a point made clear by the naval bases that the British navy maintained at Irish ports. A British "governor" continued to serve in Dublin, although the role was largely symbolic. The most powerful symbolic gesture was that Irish civil servants were required to swear the Oath of Fidelity (also known as the Oath of Allegiance) to the British Empire before they could serve. These remnants of the old relationship with England played a powerful role in the course of Irish Free State politics.

HOW DID THE IRISH CIVIL WAR CREATE ODD POLITICAL ALLIANCES IN THE IRISH FREE STATE?

The civil-war beginning of the Irish Free State accounts for the curious political divisions of twentieth-century Ireland. The fundamental political divisions in Ireland developed around those who supported the Anglo-Irish Treaty and those who opposed it, rather than on the Liberal/Conservative or Labor/Business lines seen in the political systems of most modern democratic states.

The victorious protreaty faction created a political party called Cumann na nGaedheal (KU-man na GAH-yehl), which had been the original name of Sinn Féin in 1900. Cumann na nGaedheal formed the basis of the Free State government. Its leader, William T. Cosgrave, tried to establish a stable Irish state within its constitutional boundaries as a British dominion.

But the opponents of the Anglo-Irish Treaty were still an important force. The opposing party, Fianna Fáil (fee-AH-na foil), was created in 1926 by Éamon de Valera. Fianna Fáil maintained that the provisions of the Anglo-Irish Treaty—the Oath of Fidelity and the partition of Northern Ireland—were unacceptable compromises. Although de Valera had called a halt to military opposition to the treaty, he still believed that Ireland needed to assert its independence. Fianna Fáil had limited influence in the early days because its members refused to swear the Oath of Fidelity and thus could not take their seats in the Dáil.

The priority of the Free State government under Cumann na nGaed-heal was to create a stable government. In 1924 a contingent of old IRA men within the Free State Army voiced objections to the new government. Rather than risk a military coup, the Free State government immediately removed all objectionable officers from power and placed the army under the command of a loyal Garda commander. The Irish Free State was going to be ruled by civil rather than military powers.

WHY DID THE STATUTE OF WESTMINSTER APPLY TO CANADA, INDIA, SOUTH AFRICA, *AND* THE IRISH FREE STATE?

In 1927 Fianna Fáil politicians agreed to take the Oath of Fidelity after an IRA assassination of a top Free State administrator threatened to renew factional violence. De Valera decided that the time had come to work within the constitutional framework in order to achieve his party's goals.

This strategy became increasingly effective after the British parliament passed the Statute of Westminster, which gave imperial dominions—Canada, India, South Africa, and the Irish Free State—the right to disregard parliamentary actions they did not believe should apply to them. Pushed to its logical conclusion, the Statute of Westminster effectively allowed dominions to make themselves independent in all but name.

HOW DID THE STATUTE OF WESTMINSTER CAUSE THE ECONOMIC WAR?

The 1932 general elections returned a majority of Fianna Fáil delegates to the Dáil. A few months afterward, de Valera announced that Ireland would no longer pay land annuities to England. These annuities were part of the Anglo-Irish Treaty. Farmers who had benefited from English government loans to buy land were supposed to repay the loans to the Free State government, who would then hand the money over to England. But de Valera maintained that the land had been stolen from the Irish in the first place, so Ireland had a moral justification for withholding the annuity payments.

The act was popular in Ireland, but the British Treasury was not amused. It immediately began a system of retaliatory trade measures to punish Ireland. British tariffs increased the cost of Irish cattle imports by up to 80 percent. British markets constituted 96 percent of Irish exports at this time, so the tariffs were costly, although they were partially offset by not having to pay the land annuities. This period of trade retaliation was known unofficially as the Economic War.

Withholding the land annuities was a powerful statement of independence, but Fianna Fáil wanted to go further. In 1933 it passed legislation that removed the requirement for civil servants to swear the Oath of Fidelity. Again, the British did not like to see another breach of the treaty, but the Statute of Westminster made the Irish action perfectly legal.

HOW WAS THE NATION OF
ÉIRE CREATED?

In 1936 Fianna Fáil removed references to the Crown and the British governor-general from the Irish Constitution. This was a direct challenge to the basis of the Anglo-Irish Treaty, but its reception in England was probably mitigated by the crisis over Edward VIII's abdication. In any event, it was clear that Ireland was in charge of its own constitution.

In 1937 de Valera made this point official by passing a new constitution that ended the Irish Free State of the Anglo-Irish Treaty. This new constitution established a number of key points:

- Ireland was now officially a nation called Éire.
- The nation of Éire consisted of the entire island of Ireland, including the six counties of the north.
- It allowed for religious freedom but reserved a "special relationship" with the Catholic Church.
- The constitution also created the position of an Irish president.

The first person to fill the role of president was Douglas Hyde, the scholar and patriot who forty years before had rallied Nationalist feelings around the Gaelic League.

The reaction in England was resignation. The government under Prime Minister Arthur Neville Chamberlain was unwilling to fight the move, which was, after all, technically legal under the Statute of Westminster.

The people in Northern Ireland were outraged by both the new constitution's claim to the entire island, and by the pro-Catholic position of the new country. If the two states had been far from reunification before, this step put them further apart. But by this time, de Valera and his Nationalist supporters had mostly given up hope of a near-term reunification of Ireland.

Why did Ireland stay neutral during World War II?

The great test of Irish sovereignty came in 1939, when England and Germany went to war. The United Kingdom expected that Ireland would join the war against the Axis powers. Ireland refused. In addition, de Valera refused to allow the British navy to use its former naval bases on Irish soil. In Ireland, World War II was known as "the Emergency."

The Death of Hitler

In 1945 de Valera shocked international observers by visiting the German embassy in Dublin to express his condolences on the death of Adolf Hitler. The Americans and British could not understand the gesture, but de Valera viewed it as the appropriate action for the head of a neutral state.

Ireland received a great deal of criticism for its choice of neutrality. Many English considered it a betrayal of their long-term relationship, and their government initiated an unofficial economic war of sanctions against Ireland. Americans were shocked that Ireland would not take an official stance against Germany. De Valera's government was under immense internal pressure as well, from a population whose sentiments were overwhelmingly on the side of the Allies.

But de Valera wanted to prove a point: Ireland was no longer a part of the British Empire, and the most decisive way to demonstrate that fact was to maintain firm neutrality in the war. One of the traditional arguments of the Republican movement had been that Irishmen should not have to die for another country's empire. It was a tough stance to take, but de Valera was not going to lose his chance to take it. Moreover, Ireland was in no condition to fight. Years of warfare had reduced it to a state of poverty with an army of only 7,000 poorly equipped soldiers.

HOW DID IRELAND UNOFFICIALLY SUPPORT THE ALLIED CAUSE?

Despite its official stance of neutrality, Ireland did support the Allied cause in a number of quiet ways. Thousands of Irish citizens were allowed to volunteer for Allied armies. Although downed German airmen were interned, downed Allied soldiers were promptly handed over to Northern Ireland. When Axis bombing set Belfast ablaze in 1941, de Valera promptly sent fire trucks from Dublin, Drogheda, and Dundalk to help combat the fire. Ireland also suffered its own war wounds: a German bombing raid intended for Liverpool lost its way and bombed Dublin, killing thirty-four civilians.

When the war was over, both British and American diplomats harbored resentment against Ireland's seemingly unfriendly stance. But to de Valera and his government, Ireland had demonstrated once and for all that it was in charge of its own destiny.

IRISH PROVERB

A boy's best friend is his mother and there's no spancel stronger than her apron string. (A spancel is a rope used to tie up a sheep or other animal.)

Meanwhile, Northern Ireland used the war to show its dedication to the United Kingdom. Thousands of Northern Ireland's citizens volunteered to fight. Belfast's shipbuilding industry played an important role in supplying warships for the British navy. Because of its economic importance to the Allied war effort, Belfast was the target of heavy German bombing; more than 1,200 people died in the "Belfast Blitz." Northern Ireland's sacrifices had a significant impact on its relationship with the British government in later years.

WHEN WAS THE REPUBLIC OF IRELAND CREATED?

De Valera steered Ireland through the dangerous days of World War II, but he was not the one to cut Ireland's last ties to England. In

1948, after sixteen years of Fianna Fáil dominance, Fine Gael joined with the Labour Party and a radical Nationalist group called Clann na Poblachta (KLAN-na po-BLAH-ta) to create a coalition government.

It was a strange coalition: the moderates, leftists, and nationalists of the three parties could agree on little more than a common desire to unseat Fianna Fáil. The *taoiseach* in charge of this new government was John Costello, a Dublin lawyer who had served with Fine Gael for years.

In a meeting with the prime minister of Canada in 1948, Costello revealed that Ireland intended to declare itself a republic. The following year, with a unanimous vote of the Cabinet, Ireland officially removed itself from the British Commonwealth. Ireland was now officially the Republic of Ireland. It has continued in this form to the present day.

HOW DID THE IRELAND ACT OF 1949 EFFECTIVELY DIVIDE NORTHERN IRELAND AND THE REPUBLIC OF IRELAND?

Parliament responded with the Ireland Act of 1949, which stated that Northern Ireland was still part of the United Kingdom and would remain so until the people of Northern Ireland consented to leave. This act directly contradicted the constitution of Ireland, which claimed Northern Ireland as part of the nation. In addition, the United Kingdom guaranteed to the people of Northern Ireland that their social security benefits would not be allowed to fall behind Britain's.

The effect of the Ireland Act was to seal the partition between Northern Ireland and the Republic more solidly than ever before. Politicians on both sides recognized this fact, and many criticized Costello's government for making an essentially symbolic gesture that ruined any chances of undoing Partition.

But what was done was done. The island of Ireland was now home to a British state and an independent republic, both looking anxiously across the border and wondering how they ended up so far apart.

PART 11

The Troubles

For more than three decades, a bloody conflict known as the Troubles raged in Northern Ireland. By 1999, it had claimed the lives of 3,636 people and injured 36,000 more. Most of those people were civilians. The recent success of the peace process, however, suggests that Ireland may be ready to leave tragedy behind. What do you know about the issues in Northern Ireland?

WHY DID THE FLAG AND EMBLEMS ACT NOT ALLOW NORTHERN IRELAND'S CITIZENS TO FLY THE TRICOLOR IRISH FLAG?

While the Republic of Ireland worked out its path of independent development, Northern Ireland embraced its role as a loyal province of the United Kingdom. Northern Ireland's industries successfully pursued further economic ties with England, and the standard of living in the north continued to outpace that of the south.

Northern Ireland's image as a peaceful and prosperous British province, however, concealed a tension beneath the surface. Some Irish Nationalists still wanted to undo Partition and fight for a united Ireland. Fianna Fáil maintained that Northern Ireland was part of Ireland, as shown by territorial claims in the 1937 constitution. The Protestant politicians of Northern Ireland staunchly denied these claims. In 1954 they passed the Flags and Emblems Act, which made it illegal to fly the tricolor Irish flag in Northern Ireland. Although politicians in the Republic often spoke of reuniting their country, the majority of them realized that, in practical terms, their claims were little more than rhetoric.

One group that did not accept Northern Ireland's status was the Irish Republican Army (IRA). Remnants of this organization had existed ever since the Civil War of the early 1920s, even though the Free State had outlawed it. From 1956 to 1962, IRA terrorists in the Republic waged a guerrilla war across the border against Northern Ireland's police force and soldiers. The conflict claimed nineteen lives. In the end, however, the IRA ceased the effort after it acknowledged that it had no support from the people of either the Republic or Northern Ireland.

The situation would change, however, in the late 1960s. Although Northern Ireland was generally prosperous, beneath the surface existed a profound inequality that split along religious lines. The Catholic minority of Northern Ireland was kept as an underclass by an entrenched system of discrimination in employment, housing, and education. Anger at the continuing inequality would spark a wave of civil rights protests. These protests set in motion the bloody conflict known as the Troubles.

WHY WEREN'T NORTHERN IRELAND'S CATHOLICS GIVEN EQUAL RIGHTS?

Northern Ireland was created in 1921 as a semiautonomous state, still tied to the British Empire—this was part of the agreement that Michael Collins and other Irish Nationalists made with the British. Northern Ireland ruled itself through an independent administration at Stormont, outside Belfast. The north's economic development continued to outpace the Republic of Ireland's. For nearly fifty years the region remained largely peaceful, but just beneath the orderly veneer smoldered the coals of deep-seated resentment.

Northern Ireland's approximately 550,000 Catholics never shared equally in the state's prosperity. They officially had all the rights guaranteed by the British Constitution, but unspoken rules kept them a distinct underclass. Many companies wouldn't hire Catholics, and many landlords wouldn't rent to them. Most of them worked in low-paying, unskilled jobs. Although Catholics made up 31 percent of the labor force, they only accounted for 6 percent of mechanical engineers, 8 percent of university teachers, and 19 percent of doctors.

Protestants dominated the local government and the Royal Ulster Constabulary (RUC)—the police. Northern Ireland received millions of pounds a year from the British government to invest in infrastructure, but a disproportionate amount of this money was invested in maintaining or improving Protestant areas. It was a civil rights movement waiting to happen.

HOW DID THE DERRY MARCH OF 1968 START THE TROUBLES?

The Troubles began in the late 1960s, when Catholics tried to use peaceful protest to demand equal treatment. But the Protestant population had other ideas and responded with violence. The Irish Republican Army and various Unionist paramilitary groups jumped into the fray, which quickly escalated into something resembling a local war.

In the late 1960s, a population of young, educated, and unemployed Catholics looked west and saw the success of the civil rights movement in the United States. They created the Northern Ireland

Civil Rights Association (NICRA), intending to use peaceful protest to bring attention to discrimination in employment and housing.

One of NICRA's first efforts at peaceful protest was the Derry March of 1968, which many people consider the start of the Troubles. The protesters planned to march from Belfast to Derry, imitating Martin Luther King Jr.'s 1966 march from Selma to Montgomery. The 600 marchers proceeded peacefully for four days, but when they reached Derry, a mob of Protestants attacked them with stones, nails, and crowbars. The RUC escort—which was composed primarily of Protestants—did little to protect them. Riots broke out in the Catholic Bogside neighborhood, which the RUC put down brutally.

The Derry March was an inauspicious beginning to the Unionist–Republican debate. It established an unfortunate precedent of mass violence between the sides, and it told the Catholic population that it could not trust the RUC to look after its safety. When Protestant paramilitary groups subsequently launched campaigns of arson and intimidation against them, the Catholics turned to a group that was more than willing to fight back—the IRA.

HOW DID CONFLICT BETWEEN THE IRA AND THE BRITISH GOVERNMENT ESCALATE THE VIOLENCE OF THE TROUBLES?

The IRA had kept calling for a united Ireland since the War of Independence, although its agitation hadn't been taken seriously for years.

The outbreak of violence in Derry was exactly what its members had been looking for: an excuse to strike back at the Unionists and the police forces, which the IRA saw as the agents of British imperialism.

The IRA took on the role of police and defense force for Northern Ireland's Catholics. If someone sold drugs in a Catholic neighborhood, he could be maimed or even killed by the IRA. If Unionist paramilitaries burned down a Catholic house, the IRA would bomb a Protestant pub. A stream of guns and bombs started flowing into the neighborhoods of Belfast and Derry.

The Unionist paramilitaries, meanwhile, were waging their own campaign of terror. Groups like the Ulster Defence Association (UDA) and the Red Hand Commandoes used the same tactics of murder and bombing. The UDA's attacks were generally meant to intimidate activist Catholics or to retaliate for IRA killings, which were usually in retaliation for UDA murders, which were generally retaliations for earlier IRA murders . . . and so on.

Of the paramilitary groups, the IRA always received the lion's share of news coverage, for two reasons. First, Irish descendants in other countries tended to sympathize with the IRA cause, even while condemning its methods. The news played to them. Second, the IRA chose the United Kingdom as its enemy, whereas the UDA targeted neighborhoods and individuals.

When the British government tried to control the Troubles, it moved against the group that had targeted it—the IRA. This led to increasing coverage of the IRA's role in the conflict, and it also led many Catholics to perceive that the British government was biased against their side. This perception of British bias grew much worse after one of the most notorious events of the Troubles: Bloody Sunday.

WHAT WAS BLOODY SUNDAY?

To control the increasing power of the IRA, the British government sent its army into Northern Ireland and began a policy of internment. This meant that police or soldiers could seize a suspected terrorist without formal charges and hold him or her indefinitely. By 1972, hundreds of Irish Catholics were being detained on these terms.

NICRA protested internment by holding a march through Derry's Bogside neighborhood on January 30, 1972. The local RUC chief recommended that the march be allowed to proceed as planned. An unnamed authority, however, decided instead to use the event to send in British paratroopers to arrest IRA members.

The march went on as planned and was relatively uneventful until around 4 P.M., when the soldiers arrived. They moved past the barricades and opened fire on the crowd. The march immediately dispersed in panic, and the troops followed to pursue the "arrest operation." The precise order of events that followed has been disputed for decades, but the indisputable fact is that the soldiers shot thirteen civilians dead on the spot and injured another man who later died of his wounds.

After the troops had moved out, British authorities immediately issued statements that the men killed were IRA members who had fired on the soldiers. But in the days that followed, these claims were retracted. Subsequent investigations determined that none of the men killed were carrying weapons. Investigations also failed to establish that there was any concentrated IRA presence at the scene or that the soldiers had been fired on first. What is clear is that not a single soldier was injured during the operation.

Bloody Sunday ignited Catholic fears of government bias. The British government decided that the situation in Northern Ireland had gone beyond the local government's ability to control. It suspended the Northern Ireland parliament in Stormont and imposed direct rule from London. The fifty-year experiment in Home Rule was over.

SUNDAY, BLOODY SUNDAY

By the late 1990s, new information on Bloody Sunday suggested that the soldiers had fired intentionally on unarmed civilians. It also appeared that investigators intentionally whitewashed events from the beginning—even to the point of revising soldiers' statements.

WHY WAS THE WIDGERY REPORT REFERRED TO AS THE "WIDGERY WHITEWASH"?

Bloody Sunday was the first time in the Troubles that British soldiers had opened fire on unarmed civilians. People throughout Ireland were outraged by the atrocity. On February 2, a mob attacked and burned the British embassy in Dublin, and in Australia, dockers refused to unload British cargo ships. The British government appointed Lord Widgery, lord chief justice of England, to investigate.

Widgery determined that none of the victims could be proved to have had weapons and that although some of the soldiers might have acted irresponsibly, they did not act illegally. In compiling this report, Widgery reviewed the reports of soldiers and RUC officers but ignored the statements collected from more than 500 civilians at the scene. No soldiers were punished. The Widgery report was met with outrage—some even refer to it as the "Widgery Whitewash."

How was the Council of Ireland supposed to create a lasting peace?

By 1972, Northern Ireland was in chaos: the body count from paramilitary violence was rising daily, British soldiers were patrolling the streets, and the entire state was divided along seemingly unbridgeable social lines. The British government, faced with governing this mess, began proceedings to restore Northern Ireland Home Rule on more stable grounds.

It was a gargantuan political puzzle. Negotiators had to bring together Catholic and Protestant politicians who were increasingly at each other's throats.

The negotiators ironed out an agreement in December 1973 in Sunningdale, England. The principal point was the restoration of Northern Ireland Home Rule, with power shared between Catholics and Protestants. It called for the creation of a Council of Ireland to promote cooperation between Northern Ireland and the Republic. The

English agreed to release political prisoners and reform the RUC, whereas the Irish agreed to suppress the IRA and to scale back their claims to Northern Ireland. People hoped the compromise agreement would allow for lasting peace.

How did the Ulster Workers' Council nullify the Council of Ireland?

Unionist groups felt that the compromise agreement ceded too much to Catholics. The Ulster Workers' Council, a working-class Loyalist group, called a general strike in Belfast that lasted for thirteen days. The strike—and the paramilitary violence that accompanied it—brought Northern Ireland to a standstill. The local government decided to withdraw from the Sunningdale Agreement. The United Kingdom concluded that if it couldn't reform Northern Ireland, it would try to contain it. For the next two decades, Britain treated the Troubles as primarily a security problem with the IRA.

What was the Dirty Protest?

In the following decades, the Troubles remained a source of pain and dismay for rational people throughout the world. The cycle of killing, retaliation, and counterkilling continued despite all attempts to stop it. Britain discovered that it could patrol the streets and throw thousands in jail, but so long as there was an angry young Catholic with a gun or a bomb, the violence would continue. The Catholic minority learned that they could talk to the politicians all they wanted, but so long as the Protestant working class wanted to maintain its position of superiority, the intimidation would continue. A shadow had fallen over Northern Ireland.

One of the more notorious episodes of the Troubles was the so-called Dirty Protest of IRA prisoners. The IRA prisoners wanted to be treated like prisoners of war, which would allow them to wear their own clothes, but the British insisted that they were common criminals. To protest, the prisoners refused to wear prison clothes or to clean their cells. For months, they huddled under blankets, wallowing in filth. International journalists called their conditions appalling, but British prime minister Margaret Thatcher replied that if they chose to live in squalor, that was their problem.

WHY DID IRA PRISONER BOBBY SANDS STARVE TO DEATH WHILE WAITING FOR PRISONER-OF-WAR STATUS?

In 1981, after it became clear that the dirty tactics wouldn't work, the prisoners adopted a more extreme approach. Bobby Sands, a charismatic twenty-seven-year-old prisoner, announced that he would not eat until he received prisoner-of-war status. Every ten days, a fellow prisoner joined him on the hunger strike. The British thought he was bluffing; Prime Minister Thatcher refused to give in to the moral blackmail tactics. The IRA's Gerry Adams pleaded with Sands to call off the strike, as did the Catholic bishop of Derry. While Sands wasted away, he won an election for Parliament as a Sinn Féin candidate.

But he never took his seat in Westminster. After sixty-six days without food, Bobby Sands, MP (member of Parliament), died. Riots struck throughout Belfast, and 100,000 people attended his funeral procession.

In the following months, nine more hunger strikers died. Finally, the prisoners called off the strike—they had decided not to lose any more lives in a futile gesture. Three days later, Britain granted the IRA prisoners most of their demands.

WHERE DID THE IRA GET THEIR WEAPONS?

One major source of weapons was the United States. Thousands of Irish-Americans, infuriated by what they saw as the continuing English oppression of the Irish people, gave the IRA money to buy weapons.

One of the largest shipments of weapons came from an unlikely source—Libyan dictator Colonel Gaddafi. In an attempt to destabilize the United Kingdom through terrorism, he sent the IRA four shipments of machine guns, ammunition, and explosives—hundreds of tons of weapons in all.

The supply of weapons almost certainly prolonged the conflict. The IRA maintained that it could defeat England on military grounds by making its presence in Northern Ireland so costly that England would have to pull out. The abundance of weapons made this strategy seem possible—if the IRA didn't run out of guns and bombs, it thought it could continue the campaign for as long as it took.

WHAT WAS THE ANGLO-IRISH AGREEMENT AND WHY DID IT FAIL?

A glimmer of hope came in 1985, when the United Kingdom and the Republic of Ireland tried to break through the deadlock of violence by clearing up their own interests in Northern Ireland. Prime Minister Thatcher and Garrett Fitzgerald, the *taoiseach* (Irish prime minister), signed the Anglo-Irish Agreement, which stated that "any change in the status of Northern Ireland would only come about with the consent of a majority of the people in Northern Ireland." It was a historic statement, making clear that Ulster's fate would be determined by democratic processes within Ulster, and only by those processes. The agreement also established an intergovernmental conference that gave the Republic an official consultative role in the affairs of Northern Ireland.

Although the Anglo-Irish Agreement laid the grounds for peace so far as England and the Republic were concerned, it was not well received in Northern Ireland. Unionist MPs resigned in protest, and Unionist workers called a provincewide strike. The IRA wasn't impressed either; later that year, it issued a threat of violence against all civilians, Catholic or Protestant, who worked with the RUC. The following year, a massive IRA bomb killed eleven people at a Remembrance Day ceremony in Enniskillen. Peace was not at hand.

WHY DID U.S. PRESIDENT BILL CLINTON GRANT THE HEAD OF SINN FÉIN A VISA?

For decades, it seemed that the best anyone could hope for was a contained level of violence. But a spark of hope appeared in the early 1990s when Gerry Adams, head of the IRA's political arm Sinn Féin, revealed that he'd been in peace talks with John Hume, head of the Social Democratic Labour Party (SDLP), the moderate Catholic party.

If the IRA was ready to talk, perhaps there was a chance for peace.

In January 1994, President Bill Clinton granted Gerry Adams a visa to visit the United States for the first time; previous administrations had always banned Adams because of his associations with terrorists. Adams's visit was historic for two reasons. First, it allowed him to gather the political support of Irish-Americans, which increased Sinn Féin's status in later negotiations. Second, it forced him to act as a politician, rather than as a spokesman for terrorists. He knew that if he wanted to keep the support of the United States, he needed to exchange the rifle for the negotiating table.

The IRA declared a unilateral cease-fire on August 31, 1994. In October the Unionist paramilitaries followed suit. In 1995, representatives of the United Kingdom and Ireland met to iron out a framework for a peace settlement. The document they came up with called for points similar to those in the Sunningdale Agreement:

- Northern Ireland remained part of the United Kingdom, but only so long as the majority still desired it.
- Northern Ireland would return to a form of independent government.
- The parties would create a "north–south" body that (hopefully) would lead to stronger ties between the Republic and Northern Ireland.

The framework was not an actual settlement, nor was it popular with either Republicans or Unionists. Efforts to turn the framework into an actual settlement were slow. British prime minister John Major insisted that the peace process could move forward only if the IRA agreed to decommission their arms. Gerry Adams refused; he viewed Major's position as a trick to break the IRA's power without granting any concessions.

On February 9, 1996, the IRA announced its dissatisfaction with the process by exploding an immense bomb at Canary Wharf in London. The resumption of violence was met with appalled condemnation on all sides. The British government attacked the IRA and scored a number of successes. It appeared that the nasty conflict of the 1980s and early 1990s was back again.

WHAT WAS THE GOOD FRIDAY AGREEMENT?

Fortunately, two political changes in 1997 got the peace process back on track. First, Sinn Féin won its largest percentage of the vote ever, which many interpreted as popular support for a resolution of the conflict through peaceful means. Second, Labour prime minister Tony Blair swept into power with a crushing victory over the Conservatives. Blair immediately put out feelers to Sinn Féin to get the peace process started again.

After a touch-and-go period, Prime Minister Blair brought all the major parties together in 1998. Extremists on both sides threatened to scuttle the talks, but last-minute heroics by Blair, U.S. senator George Mitchell, and President Bill Clinton kept the negotiators at the table. The Good Friday Agreement of April 10, 1998, laid the groundwork for what many hope will be a lasting peace.

The Good Friday Agreement adopted many of the provisions of previous peace attempts, such as the Sunningdale Agreement. One of the unfortunate ironies of the situation is that it took so long to reach essentially the same solution as was rejected in 1974. But maybe it took years of violence to make people accept the necessary compromises:

- ♣ Home Rule returned to Northern Ireland, with a representative assembly sharing power between Catholics and Protestants.
- ♣ The RUC was reorganized and renamed the Police Service of Northern Ireland.
- ♣ The IRA and UDA agreed to maintain the cease-fire.

♣ Assuming the cease-fire held, the IRA and UDA agreed to a gradual process of decommissioning their weapons.

♣ Political prisoners were released.

♣ The Republic of Ireland amended its constitution to remove its territorial claim to Northern Ireland until the people of Northern Ireland agreed to rejoin.

To go into effect, the agreement required the approval of a majority of the people in Northern Ireland and the Republic. In a May 1998 referendum, it drew the support of 94.4 percent of voters in the Republic and 71.1 percent of people in Northern Ireland. Although this result gave a great boost to the peace process, one element of the vote still gave people pause: 96 percent of Catholic voters in Northern Ireland supported the Good Friday Agreement, but only 52 percent of Protestants voted in favor.

HOW IS THE PEACE IN NORTHERN IRELAND TESTED ON A YEARLY BASIS?

Although the leaders have decided to move forward, a great deal of anger remains in the people of Northern Ireland. Every summer the peace is tested in the Marching Season, when the Orange Order and Apprentice Boy parades antagonize Catholic neighborhoods. These Unionist groups march through Catholic neighborhoods on dates significant to their history, such as the Protestant victory in the Battle of the Boyne.

The Orange Order claims that the marches are part of its cultural heritage; Catholics claim they are triumphalist gestures designed to humiliate them. In an attempt to prevent Catholic riots, the newly installed Parades Commission has voted to prevent marches through traditionally troubled areas. The resulting police blockades have sparked Protestant riots.

THE ORANGE ORDER AND THE APPRENTICE BOYS

The Orange Order is named in honor of William of Orange, the British king who defeated James II in the battles of the Boyne and Aughrim (1690–91). William's victory sealed Protestant domination over Ireland for the next two centuries. The Apprentice Boys are named after a group of apprentices who sealed the gates of Derry against James II's army.

WHAT IS THE POLITICAL STRUCTURE IN IRELAND LIKE TODAY?

The Irish political structure continues to be something of an anomaly, because the two dominant parties are divided less by ideology than by historical associations. Fianna Fáil, the party founded by Éamon de Valera and the forces who opposed the Anglo-Irish Treaty, has been the dominant party throughout the century. Fine Gael, the organization that emerged from the Free State politicians who supported the treaty, has managed to take control of the government on a number of occasions with the help of third parties. The major political parties in Ireland today are:

- ♣ **Fianna Fáil:** the original antitreaty party
- ♣ **Fine Gael:** the original protreaty party
- ♣ **Labour:** a liberal workers' party
- ♣ **Progressive Democrats:** an offshoot of Fianna Fáil that is economically conservative and socially liberal; it has allied with Fine Gael at times
- ♣ **Democratic Left:** the modern incarnation of the original Sinn Féin; leftist but no longer socialist
- ♣ **Greens:** an environmental party

PART 12

Irish Song, Dance, and Storytelling

By the end of the seventeenth century, England's political domination of Ireland was complete. Although the English tried to force their language and religion onto Ireland, the Irish culture proved resilient and Irish songs, dances, and storytelling traditions continued unabated. How much do you know about the rich cultural history of Ireland?

WHY ISN'T IRISH STILL SPOKEN PROMINENTLY?

The Gaelic language of Ireland is one of the most distinctive in Europe. It's one of the few Celtic languages that survived the onslaught of Germanic and Latin tongues. Some of the oldest vernacular literature in Europe was composed in Irish, and an extraordinary range of Irish stories survived into the modern day. Irish is a lyrical language that seems particularly well suited to poetry and metaphor. But it's lucky to be around today. We have the efforts of many generations of stubborn Irish people to thank for its modern existence.

In 1500, the great majority of Ireland's inhabitants still spoke Irish as their first language. The Anglo-Norman families like the FitzGeralds and Butlers spoke both English and Irish, but the farmers and laborers outside the Pale spoke predominantly Irish. With the plantations and conquests of the sixteenth and seventeenth centuries, however, the language trends began to change.

Thousands of English-speaking families moved onto Irish land. English policies actively promoted the adoption of the English language. A story says that schoolteachers hung sticks from students' necks and notched them every time the students spoke Irish; for every notch the student received a beating. The most powerful force against Irish was the fact that all the wealthy and powerful people spoke English, so a person needed to speak English to have any opportunities for advancement. Between 1700 and 1900, Irish went from being the majority language of the island to a minor tongue spoken by disenfranchised groups in the West.

The Irish were pressured to speak English, but it was hard for them to learn to read it. The penal laws prevented most Irish children from attending school. But the Irish had a resourceful response to this problem; they created hedge schools—informal schools taught in the open or in barns by volunteer schoolteachers. These schools taught English, Irish, Latin, history, geography, and whatever else they could manage. They didn't have many books and couldn't meet all the time, but they did prevent the Irish people from becoming totally illiterate.

Although it suffered, the Irish language didn't die out. It lived on in remote places with little English presence, particularly in the west. The English didn't bother to put schools in backward outposts like the Blasket Islands off the Dingle coast. The province of Connacht, which Cromwell had seen fit to leave to the Irish, remained the bastion of the old Gaelic language. The area where Irish continued to be spoken as a first language was called the Gaeltacht.

Over the years, the Irish government has instituted a number of programs to preserve the Irish language. Irish is the official language of the Republic of Ireland and a mandatory part of the curriculum for all Irish schoolchildren. For a while, all civil servants had to pass examinations in Irish before they could take their posts. The government has provided a number of incentives to promote Irish-language initiatives in the Gaeltacht, such as Raidió na Gaeltachta, an all-Irish radio station.

What's so important about Irish music?

A major upsurge of interest in traditional Irish music has occurred in recent years. Bands such as the Chieftains and Clannad have helped develop a worldwide interest in the lyrical sound of Celtic music. Musicians throughout Ireland and its emigrant communities have found opportunities to play for adoring crowds in Irish pubs everywhere. These musicians are continuing in a Celtic music tradition that goes back many centuries.

A Fleadh in Ennis

The best way to hear a range of traditional Irish music is to attend a *Fleadh* (flah), a traditional music festival. These festivals attract musicians and dancers from all over Ireland. The largest festival, the Fleadh Nua, is held over a five-day period every May in a small town named Ennis in County Clare.

Poets and bards were big shots in Celtic societies. A good poet could grant either fame or shame to Celtic nobles, so when one showed up at court and started to sing, everyone gathered to listen. These bards often played harps and other musical instruments. Brian Boru's harp—the symbol of Ireland—was supposedly played to rally his troops.

The singing poets continued their cultural influence after the Norman Conquest. The Anglo-Norman nobles, like the old Irish nobles before them, recognized the power of a good song, so they often sponsored these bards in their courts. Over time, however, the power of the bards waned. With books and letters available, nobles no longer needed poets to spread their fame.

Irish music is a free-form style. The length, pace, and musical composition of a given piece will change from night to night and from group to group. Traditional musicians almost never play from written music; in the past, many of the best musicians couldn't even read music. As in American jazz, most pieces revolve around group performances that highlight the virtuosic improvisations of individual musicians.

Despite the free-form style, Irish music has a distinctive sound that makes it immediately identifiable (although Scottish and Welsh music sound similar). The distinctiveness comes largely from the mix of instruments used. The traditional instruments of Irish music are:

- Harp
- Bodhrán drum
- Fiddle
- Flute
- Tin whistle
- Accordion
- Bagpipes or uilleann pipes

Traditional music performances are informal. They generally take place in pubs, with the musicians performing for free beer and the cheers of the crowd. Members of the audience can join in if they have a fiddle, a good voice, or even just a set of spoons to add to the music.

WHO WROTE "DANNY BOY"?

The Irish love of poetic language has mixed with humor and tragedy to produce the beautiful Irish ballad. The ability to compose and perform a beautiful ballad has been highly prized in Ireland for centuries. The ballad is generally sung by a single person, who may or may not be accompanied by instruments. Ballads range from a handful of lines to many hundreds of lines in length. They can tell stories of lost love, injustice and revenge, or what happened when the singer went to get a beer.

Surprisingly, the lyrics to one favorite Irish ballad, "Danny Boy," weren't even written by an Irishman. An Englishman named Frederic Weatherly composed them in 1910. The music is from an older tune called "Londonderry Air," which was transcribed by Jane Ross of County Derry around 1855. The origins of "Londonderry Air" are unclear, but some claim that it was a traditional harp song.

HOW IMPORTANT IS DANCE TO IRISH CULTURE?

Dancing has been an important form of artistic expression and social interaction in Ireland for thousands of years. The Celts and the druids had their own forms of folk dancing. Some say that the prevalence of ring structures in modern Irish dancing has to do with the way the ancient druids danced around sacred oak trees—either that, or it's just easier to dance in a circle.

The Vikings, the Normans, and the English all probably contributed to the development of dance in Ireland. By the sixteenth century, three dances were spoken of as distinctively Irish: the Irish Hey, the Rinnce Fada, and the Trenchmore. Sir Henry Sidney, Queen Elizabeth's lieutenant in Ireland, saw some comely Irish lasses dancing Irish jigs in Galway. He wrote, "They are very beautiful, magnificently dressed and first class dancers." Whenever royalty or important guests visited Ireland, it was customary to meet them with fancy dancers.

The development of contemporary Irish dance is unclear. It is known, however, that dancing was an important part of the social lives of the native Irish population. Festivals, weddings, and wakes were all occasions for dancing. Towns held dance competitions, and wandering dance masters went from town to town, teaching all the latest steps. Through the influence of these itinerant masters the Irish forms of the jig, reel, hornpie, and polka developed.

Today, thanks in part to *Riverdance*, Irish step-dancing is the most recognizable form of Irish dance. In this style, dancers hold a rigid posture, keep their arms mostly by their sides, and step and kick about for all they're worth. Many Irish dancers maintain that their ancestors developed this rigid-armed style of dancing so that if English people looked in through a window they wouldn't be able to tell that the Irish were dancing. There may be a grain of truth to this, but most dance scholars think the style was adapted from French dances imported in the eighteenth century.

The most authentically Irish form of dance is the *céilí*, or *ceilidh* (KAY-lee), which is similar in form to folk dancing in many other parts of the world. A *céilí* is essentially a dance party in which everyone dances to traditional Irish music, spinning, exchanging partners, waltzing around, and generally having a good time. *Céilí* dance arrangements usually involve four or more dancers at a time. Irish-American organizations throughout the United States host *céilís* from time to time.

WHY ARE IRISH WAKES
SO MUCH FUN?

For the Irish, a funeral isn't just an occasion for mourning. It is also an opportunity to get together with friends, meet members of the opposite sex, and play wild games. This both honors the dead person and allows the living to rejoice in their continuing lives.

Traditionally the corpse and his or her family were separated from the party by a screen so that the mourners could grieve and weep without distraction. Meanwhile, all the guests drank whiskey, sang, smoked, and played various party games. These games involved mock marriages and some games that the clergy condemned as downright obscene—not unlike the games played at some teenage parties today.

WHO ARE THE WEE FOLK?

The Irish people have maintained a set of unique beliefs and superstitions that live on into the modern day. An abundance of stories and superstitions exists about the mischief of the fairies. The Irish term for the fairies is *sídhe* (shee); in English they are called by a number of terms, such as "wee folk" or the "good people." Irish legends suggest an extraordinary diversity of charming and terrifying fairies frolic in the countryside:

- **Changelings:** fairy children left in place of stolen mortal babies; the fairies were said to leave sickly babies after stealing healthy ones.
- **Bean sídhe (banshee):** a female spirit associated with the ancestors of old Irish families, who wails terribly whenever someone in the family dies.
- **Gruagach:** a female spirit that guards livestock but requires an offering of milk.
- **Selkies:** gentle spirits that can shape-shift from seals to humans; they sometimes marry humans.
- **Lianhan shee:** a sort of love goddess who invites men for trysts in Tír na nÓg (the home of the fairies); loving the Lianhan shee almost invariably results in disaster.
- **Leprechauns:** short, mischievous creatures known for their skills in making shoes and hiding gold; if a mortal traps one at the end of a rainbow, he or she can take the leprechaun's pot of gold.
- **Cluricauns:** similar to leprechauns, except they don't make shoes; they like to steal shepherds' dogs and goats for impromptu midnight races.
- **Pooka:** a spooky spirit who appears as a black eagle, goat, or horse; he has the irritating habit of picking up unwary travelers for terrifying midnight rides, sometimes into the sea.

It is widely suspected that the fairies came from one of the races that inhabited Ireland before the Celts arrived. Numerous rings of stones can be found throughout the Irish countryside—local legend generally attributes these "fairy rings" to Ireland's mystical inhabitants from the past. Superstitious locals have avoided the rings for centuries.

Less superstitious archaeologists usually attribute the rings to Ireland's Stone Age inhabitants.

HOW CAN YOU PLACATE FAIRIES, FIND LOVE AND WEALTH, AND AVERT DISASTER?

The beauty of Irish superstitions is that the Irish adopted all the superstitions of Christian culture without giving up their old Celtic beliefs. This resulted in a cornucopia of beliefs about how to avert disaster, placate the fairies, or attain wealth and love.

A great many superstitions dealt with relations with the spirit world. The wee folk were considered notoriously mischievous, so a wise person kept a number of practices in mind—only calling them "the good people," for example. People called out a warning whenever they threw water out of the house, for fear of hitting an unsuspecting fairy. To stay on the fairies' good sides, sensible housewives always left out plates of food or milk for the little people to enjoy. If someone should be so unfortunate as to cross paths with hostile fairies, it was well known that throwing dust from under one's feet would force the fairies to give up any human captives. When gathering wood for a fire, people would never take anything growing on a fairy mound.

A number of beliefs dealt with specific holidays. On Halloween it was customary to put up Parshell crosses—two sticks tied together with twine—to keep spirits at bay (the Parshell cross looks suspiciously like the spooky sticks in the film *The Blair Witch Project*). On Beltane, May 1, a woman could achieve great beauty by rolling naked in the morning dew. St. Stephen's Day—December 26—was also known as Wren Day because local boys would hunt down a wren and then parade it around town on a stick for good luck. On Whit Sunday, celebrated seven days after Easter Sunday, it was considered unwise to go anywhere near water, because it was widely known that the spirits of drowned people rose up on that day and tried to pull down the living.

WHAT POPULAR IRISH SPORT WAS ONCE USED TO TRAIN WARRIORS?

The Celts were an active, warlike folk, so when they found themselves at peace, they invented warlike sports to keep themselves fit. Although they'd beaten their Celtic swords into plowshares, Irish farmers continued to play these exciting sports. In the late nineteenth century, the Gaelic Athletic Association (GAA) officially revived them. GAA matches still gather roaring crowds from across the island.

One of the most unique Irish sports is hurling, an ancient game played by two 15-member teams armed with curved wooden sticks called "hurlies." Players use the sticks to smack around a hard leather ball (*sliothar*), at speeds of up to 80 miles per hour, until it goes through a hoop. With all the swinging and smacking, injuries are common; it's said that the ancient Celts used the sport as a training tool to give their warriors strong bones. The All-Ireland Hurling

Final, held every year at Croke Park in Dublin, excites fanatical enthusiasm.

The women's version of hurling is called *camogie*. Camogie matches tend to be somewhat less violent than the men's matches, but they are popular anyway.

Hurling is an ancient sport, and forms of it have evolved into a number of popular modern sports. The Scottish form of hurling is called *shinty*. Because shinty involves hitting a ball around with a stick, it is thought to have inspired that other Scottish sport, golf. Hurling and shinty enthusiasts who emigrated to Canada adapted their favorite sports to the ice and called it hockey. Unlike the Celts or the Irish, however, the Canadians had the sense to wear pads.

A marginally safer form of hurling evolved into Gaelic football, the GAA's other major sport. It's kind of like soccer, except the players use their hands. It's also kind of like rugby, and the players don't wear pads. Games are fast and furious.

HOW DID *SEANACHAÍS* SPIN YARNS?

Irish storytellers are famous for their wit and inventiveness. The extraordinary range of Irish stories comes from a folklore tradition more than 2,000 years old, which successfully blended Celtic, Christian, and English influences to create some of the most distinctive oral literature in all of Europe. Although the traditional format for Irish storytelling is dying out, its legacy continues in books and in poetry.

Ireland has one of the richest folklore traditions in the world. Folklorists have hypothesized that in 1935 the parish of Carna, in west Galway, held more unrecorded folktales than did the rest of Western Europe combined.

The reasons for this rich heritage are many, but two main factors stand out. First, Irish culture kept a Celtic base for more than 2,000 years, while incorporating the traditions and beliefs of Christianity, the Vikings, the Normans, and the English. These layers of culture piled on top of one another to create a rich tapestry. Second, the tradition of oral composition and performance has been strong in Ireland throughout the years.

In ancient Celtic society, professional singers and poets called bards were extremely important. The Celts didn't write, so bards memorized vast amounts of poetry and performed it live. Their poems and songs were often the only record of a king's deeds or misdeeds, and their performances were the best entertainment around. People were accustomed to listening to stories told aloud and appreciated skilled storytellers.

As time went on, more people learned to read and write and the bards became less important. But the Irish populace remained mostly illiterate, so they kept up the tradition of oral storytelling. Bards evolved into wandering storytellers called *shanachies*, or *scanachaí* (SHAN-uck-ee), who went from town to town, entertaining the townsfolk. *Shanachies*, like their bard predecessors, were always welcome; people paid them with food if money wasn't available. When there wasn't a *shanachie* around, ordinary people entertained themselves by telling stories around the fire.

A good storyteller knew hundreds of tales and could perform them with gusto and eloquence. In this informal way, an ancient oral literary tradition quietly continued into modern times.

How did the brothers Grimm help record Irish folklore?

For centuries, Irish folktales were unknown to the outside world. During the Protestant Ascendancy, the ruling class had nothing but disdain for the stories of Irish farmers. Not only were most of the stories in the Irish tongue, but also they were all about fantastic heroes and fairies, which the English dismissed as a bunch of superstitious nonsense.

In the early nineteenth century, folklore suddenly became fashionable. The Brothers Grimm in Germany started collecting and studying folktales (which you can read in *Grimm's Fairy Tales*) and declared folklore a vital expression of a culture's heritage. Soon, enterprising Irish scholars began to explore the countryside, looking for stories of value. They found a gold mine.

The first volume of Irish folktales was *Fairy Legends and Traditions of the South of Ireland*, published in 1825 by Thomas Croker from Cork. Croker and other early scholars of Irish folklore visited the Anglicized areas of Ireland in the east and recorded only the stories that were told to them in English. This limited the value of their work because it ignored the great majority of Irish folktales, which were told only in Irish.

In the mid-nineteenth century, Jeremiah Curtin, an Irish-American who had learned Irish, traveled throughout the Irish-speaking enclaves in Connacht and discovered hundreds of previously unrecorded stories. He recorded and published them in their original language and greatly advanced the study of Irish folklore.

HOW DID OSCAR WILDE'S PARENTS KEEP THE ART OF STORYTELLING ALIVE?

At the end of the nineteenth century, Irish folklore studies became respectable. Oscar Wilde's parents, Sir William and Speranza Wilde (Speranza was Mrs. Wilde's pen name; her real name was Jane Francesca), were important figures in this field and eccentric luminaries on the Anglo-Irish scene.

The intellectuals of the Celtic Renaissance drew their inspiration from the Irish language and its folklore. Douglas Hyde's *Beside the Fire*, William Butler Yeats's *The Celtic Twilight*, Lady Augusta Gregory's *Visions and Beliefs of the West of Ireland*, and Standish O'Grady's collections not only established Irish folklore as one of the great oral literature traditions of Western civilization, but also provided an immense source of pride for the growing Irish Nationalist movement.

Even as Yeats and Lady Gregory collected tales in the cottages of Sligo and Connemara, they recognized that the storytelling tradition was dying out. They knew that if the Irish language died, a vast literary heritage would die with it. To prevent that from happening, in 1935 the Irish government created the Irish Folklore Commission. In the following decades, Irish-speaking collectors scoured the countryside to record stories of saints, heroes, and spirits. Currently, more than 1.5 million pages of folklore reside in the commission's collection, which since 1971 has been continued by the Folklore Department at University College Dublin.

WHY DO PEOPLE KISS THE BLARNEY STONE?

The Irish genius for glib speech and storytelling is called the gift of gab. To acquire this eloquence for yourself, all you have to do is kiss the Blarney Stone, also known as the Stone of Eloquence, at Blarney Castle in County Cork.

Legend has it that the builder of Blarney Castle, Cormac Laidir MacCarthy, was involved in a lawsuit during the castle's construction. The night before he appeared in court to plead his case, he said a prayer to the goddess Cliodhna, the queen of the banshees, and asked for her help. She responded by telling MacCarthy to kiss the first stone he saw the next day on his way to the courthouse. MacCarthy kissed a huge chunk of bluestone and walked away from the hearing the victor. To praise Cliodhna and preserve the power of the stone that he kissed, MacCarthy had the stone incorporated in the parapet of Blarney Castle.

The power of the stone was memorialized by Francis Sylvester Mahoney, an Irish bard who wrote:

There is a stone there, that whoever kisses,
Oh! He never misses to grow eloquent:
'Tis he may clamber to a lady's chamber,
Or become a member of Parliament.

Over the years, millions of tourists, authors, and statesmen have kissed the Blarney Stone looking for a bit of MacCarthy's eloquence, but it's not so easy to access the stone's gift of gab. First you have to climb 127 steep steps to the top of the castle's walls. There, thirty-seven feet up, is the Stone. To kiss it, you have to lean back over the empty space in the wall while lying on your back. Today, an iron railing and the capable hands of a Blarney Castle employee ensure that you won't fall off the parapet—but that wasn't the case until recently and kissers have, indeed, fallen to their deaths in the pursuit of the gift of gab.

HOW CAN YOU CATCH A LEPRECHAUN?

The leprechaun is perhaps the most famous of Ireland's little people. In one story, a man came down from his fields one day and went to look after his old mare that had served him well for many years. When he approached the stable, he heard a loud hammering sound. He peeked through a window and spotted a funny little man sitting under his mare, hammering away at some shoes and whistling the prettiest tune the man had ever heard. He realized what he had in his stable—a leprechaun.

Leprechauns are famous for their shoemaking abilities, but they're even more famous for their gold. The man knew this, so he snuck in the back door and tiptoed up behind the little fellow. The leprechaun was so busy making his shoes that he didn't notice the man until the man had caught the leprechaun. "I have you now," the man said, "and I won't let you go until I have your gold!"

"Stop, you're squeezing too hard!" said the leprechaun. "Let me go for a moment and I'll get you the gold." Eager for the gold, the man released the leprechaun, who, quick as a wink, ran out the door. All the man had left was the little shoe that the leprechaun had been making.

The man didn't get any gold, but his wife said that it was the prettiest shoe she'd ever seen.

WHAT HAPPENS WHEN YOU GET A FLORIN FROM A FAIRY?

Some fairies are thought to be helpful, in their own mysterious ways. One story tells of a man who started feeling faint while in church. He walked outside to clear his head, and a gentleman approached to ask if he was all right. The churchgoer explained that he was feeling faint. The gentleman handed him a florin (a valuable coin) and told him to go have a whiskey at the local pub (Irish whiskey, of course, has amazing curative powers). The man thanked him and walked to the pub.

He paid for his drink with the florin, took the change, and drank down the whiskey. In no time at all he was feeling better. The man went home thinking nothing of it.

The next day he was going fishing, so he went to the store to buy some tobacco for his trip. When he reached into his pocket to get some money, he was surprised to find that the same florin was in his pocket. He paid with the florin, took the change, and walked away smoking, wondering what had happened. On the way home after fishing, he stopped by the bakery for some bread. He discovered that the same florin was in his pocket again.

The man continued in this way for some time, paying for everything with the florin and always finding it back in his pocket. He was happy with his good fortune, but something about the strange coin never seemed right to him. One day he went into the pub where he'd bought the first glass of whiskey. He threw the florin down on the counter and yelled, "May the devil go with you!"

He never saw the coin again. To the end of his days, he always said that a fairy man had given it to him.

WHY DO IRISH CATS SLEEP INSIDE?

An Irish story explains why cats get to stay inside by the fire while dogs have to sleep out in the cold. Long ago, a cat and a dog argued over who would get to stay inside. Their owner overheard the argument and decided to settle the matter.

"We'll have a race," he said. "You'll start five miles from the house, and whoever gets to the house first can stay inside the house from then on. The other can look after the place outside."

So the next day the two animals went to the place where the race was to start. They both ran as fast as they could. The dog, with his longer legs, got far ahead of the cat. But an old beggar saw the dog running at him with his mouth open, and he thought the dog was going to bite him. The beggar hit the dog with a stick. The dog was angry, so he barked at the man and tried to bite him for satisfaction.

When the dog finally got to the house, the cat was licking her paws by the fire. From that day on, cats have stayed inside the house while dogs have slept outside in the cold.

PART 13

Sláinte! Food and Drink in Ireland

The Irish family has traditionally gathered around the table, sharing the food it had in rich times and in poor. For the most part, it has been pretty decent fare. Ireland's thriving agricultural industry provides high-quality meat, dairy products, and vegetables that go directly to local markets. The fresh and nutritious ingredients have allowed the Irish population to stay remarkably healthy, even in times of relative poverty. What do you know about Ireland's food and drink?

Does Ireland have a national dish?

Irish food has never been known for its diversity. The traditional diet, consisting of meat, vegetables, and lots and lots of potatoes, has long been considered one of the blandest in Europe. What it lacks in flair, though, it makes up for in heartiness. Some of Ireland's substantial national and regional dishes include the following:

- ♣ **Blaa ("blah"):** sausage rolls, from Waterford
- ♣ **Coddle:** boiled sausages and bacon with potatoes, from Dublin
- ♣ **Colcannon:** a casserole of potatoes, onions, and cabbage
- ♣ **Crubeen:** pig's feet, from Cork
- ♣ **Guinness stew:** a stew made with mutton, potatoes, carrots, and Guinness beer
- ♣ **Soda bread:** a thick brown bread, tasty when fried

Do the Irish really eat blood sausage?

The Irish tend to eat light lunches, so they take breakfast seriously. Visitors to Ireland are frequently amazed by the robust Irish breakfast. This is no dainty continental breakfast of a croissant and jam, but an extravaganza of meat and eggs that will keep you full all day. You'll find some variation from place to place, but the Irish breakfast generally includes the following:

- Eggs (usually fried)
- White pudding (a lighter sausage)
- Sausages
- Fried tomatoes
- Bacon (sliced thick)
- Toast and jam
- Ham
- Tea
- Black pudding (a blood sausage)

This combination is served in pubs and bed-and-breakfasts across the country. A similar variant, called an "Ulster Fry," is served in the north. Observant visitors will notice that the Irish don't actually eat like this every day; a bowl of cereal or some toast and tea are more common ways to start the day.

DO THE IRISH LOVE A SPOT OF TEA?

It's hard to overestimate the importance of tea in Irish culture. Tea is simultaneously a beverage, a medicine, and a social ritual. The Irish drink on average four cups of tea a day, amounting to 7 pounds of dried tea leaves over the course of a year—easily the highest rate of per-capita tea consumption in the world. No respectable household would be found without tea, and pubs are legally required to provide it. At breakfast, lunch, and teatime (approximately 4 P.M.), tea is the beverage of choice.

The Anglo-Irish aristocracy introduced tea to Ireland in the nineteenth century. As an import from India, it was too expensive for most Irish people at first, but lower prices and generally improving economic conditions allowed more and more people to try this new taste sensation. Soon the whole nation was hooked. They pronounced the name of their new drink "tay," from the French pronunciation.

WHAT'S A CUPPA?

A cup of tea is often referred to as a "cuppa"—and everyone knows what kind of cup you're talking about. People throughout the country take a break in the midafternoon to enjoy a cup of tea and some light snacks such as cookies or finger sandwiches. The Irish drink tea with sugar and generous amounts of milk. Tea devotees extol the drink's powers to aid digestion, cure headaches, and provide a gentle pick-me-up.

WHERE DOES IRISH TEA COME FROM?

The Irish tend to prefer stronger tea than the English—they have a saying that a good cup of tea should be "strong enough for a mouse to trot on." They've gravitated toward East African suppliers, who provide more aromatic leaves. Irish tea was traditionally made using free leaves, but in recent decades consumers have grown more accepting of tea bags. The Irish maintain very high standards for their tea; consequently, the quality of tea in Ireland is generally much higher than in the United States.

The Irish initially relied entirely on U.K. importers for their tea supply, which became a problem during World War II, when Ireland chose not to ally itself with the United Kingdom. Consequently, the government of Ireland set up Tea Importers (Éire), Ltd., a conglomeration of companies that imported tea directly from the producing countries.

INÒIAN BREAKFAST TEA?

Irish breakfast tea, available from tea purveyors everywhere, is a blend of black teas from the Assam region of India. It contains dark brown leaves that brew a hearty, malty, deep red tea that takes milk and sugar very well—perfect for breakfast!

Irish tea consumption continued to increase in the postwar years. In 1973 Ireland had to disband Tea Importers because it violated anti-monopoly statutes of the EU, so the business was taken up by the subsidiary companies that had made up the organization.

WHY ARE THERE KIDS IN IRISH PUBS?

Pubs play a very important role in Irish life. American visitors tend to assume that pubs are the same thing as bars, but this isn't exactly true.

Pubs do sell alcohol, but they also serve as restaurants, music stages, meeting places, and even as local cultural museums. Most pubs aren't all these things simultaneously, but instead specialize in one area.

One thing that often surprises visitors is the presence of children and families in Irish pubs. The drinking age in Ireland is eighteen, but it's legal for children under that age to enter with their families. The families are there for the music or the food. Irish pub food—called "pub grub"—is generally inexpensive and hearty. Almost any pub can be expected to provide sandwiches or maybe a baked potato; however, some pubs have become famous for their food.

ḃAVE SOᗰE CRÁIC!

"Pub" is short for "public house." The person who runs a pub is called a "publican." All pubs offer beer, but the most important thing for a pub to offer is *cráic* (pronounced "crack"), which is Irish for a jolly good time!

Pubs are the places to go for traditional music, or "trad," as the locals call it. Larger places might bring in professional bands, but the most common format is the session, in which local musicians come with what instruments they have and just get down to business. The musicians in a session are usually playing for beer only, so there generally isn't a cover charge. The pubs in Doolin, County Clare, are famous for their trad.

WHY IS GUINNESS SO POPULAR?

Ireland has one of the highest beer consumption rates in the world. The unique thing about Irish beer habits is that the most popular type of beer is stout, whereas all other European markets prefer lagers or ales. The most famous stout, of course, is Guinness.

If you stop at a pub in Ireland and ask for a pint, the bartender will invariably bring you a Guinness. This unspoken understanding demonstrates the centrality of Guinness in Irish pub culture. Guinness stout is not only the national drink, it is also one of Ireland's leading exports; in recent years Guinness has sold close to 2 billion pints of stout per year in more than 150 different countries.

Arthur Guinness started the first Guinness brewery in 1759 with the help of a £100 inheritance from his godfather, the archbishop of Cashel. A man with vision, Guinness took out a 9,000-year lease on a run-down brewery on St. James Street in Dublin, right next to the Liffey River. This location was crucial, because it ensured a ready supply of pure Irish spring water. Guinness was a big fan of porter, as stout was called then, and he dedicated his new brewery to producing it. After some experimentation he found a taste that people loved, and the business has been growing ever since.

Like most beers, Guinness is made from barley, hops, yeast, and water (originally from the St. James wells in County Kildare). Guinness's distinctive flavor and dark color come from the practice of roasting the hops before brewing them. The beer isn't black, as many people think, but actually a deep ruby color—you can see the true color by holding your pint up to the light.

HOW DO YOU POUR THE PERFECT PINT?

A proper pint of Guinness should have a thick head of foam on top. To get this right, the bartender pours the draft into the pint, lets it sit for three or four minutes, then tops it off for serving. Traditionally, Guinness stout was served at room temperature. (Irish room temperature can be pretty cool, so that doesn't mean the beer was warm.) Some pubs in Ireland continue that practice. There used to be a big difference between the flavors of draft Guinness and bottled Guinness, but recent advances in packaging technology have produced cans that can pour a pint almost as good as you'd find in a pub in County Meath.

There is considerable dispute in Ireland about where you can find the best pint. In Dublin, the two leading contenders are the St. James Gate Brewery and Mulligan's, a nearby pub that, according to folklore, has a pipe connecting its basement to the brewery. Other Irish people claim that you'll find the best pint in little pubs out in the country that serve their beer at room temperature and never clean the tap.

ARE THERE OTHER IRISH BEERS?

Guinness gets the lion's share of attention, but Ireland produces a number of other excellent beers. Brewers in Cork make Murphy's and Beamish, stouts that appear similar to Guinness but have distinctly different flavors. In Cork and the rest of Munster, these local brews are often more popular than Guinness stout. You can occasionally find Murphy's in bars outside of Ireland.

Smithwicks ("Smiddicks") is the local brew in Kilkenny. Smithwicks is an amber ale with a slightly hoppy flavor. It's served throughout Ireland. In continental Europe, you might find it under the name "Kilkenny."

A number of other beers have recently come on the market to take advantage of the international enthusiasm for Irish beer. Harp is a lager brewed by Guinness. Murphy's has started brewing an ale called Murphy's Irish Red. With the proliferation of Irish pubs around the world, expect more Irish beers to appear in the near future.

WHAT'S THE DIFFERENCE BETWEEN "WHISKEY" AND "WHISKY"?

Queen Elizabeth I of England once remarked that her only true Irish friend was whiskey. The word "whiskey" comes from the Gaelic words *uisce beatha,* which mean "water of life." The origins of whiskey are lost in the mists of time; some historians think the distilling technology was developed in the Far East and brought to Scotland and Ireland by traveling Celts. By 1000 c.e. people in both Scotland and Ireland were fermenting grains, distilling the brew, and aging the final product in wooden barrels.

Modern Irish whiskey is similar to Scotch whisky, but it's distilled three times instead of two, it's slightly sweeter, has less peat flavor, and it's spelled with an "e"—Scotch is spelled "whisky." Although Scotch whisky enjoys a far larger market today, in the nineteenth century Irish whiskey was the more popular drink. It was the liquor of choice in Victorian England, but in the period from 1910 to 1945 the Irish whiskey industry hit on hard times when the combination of Irish independence, American Prohibition, trade disputes with England, and World War II effectively ruined the export market.

Nevertheless, the domestic Irish market managed to keep a few distillers alive. The Bushmill's distillery in the north continued to produce Bushmill's malt whiskey, and the Midleton distillery near Cork produced the Jameson, Powers, and Midleton whiskies.

In recent years, Ireland's tourist boom has encouraged entrepreneurs to revive old Irish brands and distilleries. Today, there are dozens of Irish whiskey brands on the market, including Paddy, Kilbeggan, Locke's, Tullamore Dew, Redbreast, and Greenore.

IS IT LEGAL TO BREW POTEEN?

A discussion of Irish distilled beverages would not be complete without a mention of poteen, *poitín* (po-CHEEN) in Irish Gaelic, an extremely strong grain alcohol made in unlicensed stills in the country—like moonshine. It's said that farmers used to give *poitín* to cows in labor. Supposedly, you can still find it in remote rural areas, but we don't recommend that you drink it; the ethyl alcohol in bad batches can be poisonous.

PART 14

Irish Literature

Irish writers have made extraordinary contributions to English literature, producing four Nobel Prize winners. Although many of Ireland's greatest writers left their island to work in other countries, their work demonstrates the love of wit and poetry that has characterized the Irish people for centuries. What do you know about Ireland's literary bards?

WHY DID IRISH WRITERS IMMIGRATE TO ENGLAND?

The full story of Irish literature begins long before the English ever arrived in Ireland. The Celtic epics such as the *Taín Bó Cuailnge*, represent one of the great oral literary traditions in world history. In the Middle Ages, Irish bards were famous for the originality of their poetry. It is very unfortunate that relatively little of that poetry survives today.

Few Irish writers stood out during the years of English domination. After all, most of the Irish were uneducated farmers who had little opportunity to express themselves in writing. Moreover, the most talented writers went to England to pursue the greater opportunities there. This trend of writers leaving the country has continued into the modern day.

In the last 150 years, however, the growth of Irish consciousness has created a greater distinction between the cultures of Ireland and England, in the minds of both the Irish and the rest of the world. This distinction has allowed people to talk about a body of Irish literature that can stand shoulder-to-shoulder with the literature of England or the United States.

WHAT IRISH AUTHOR USED SATIRE TO BECOME A NATIONAL HERO?

Ireland's first great contributor to English literature was Jonathan Swift. Born in Dublin to Protestant English parents, Swift faced financial challenges after his father's early death. After an education at Trinity College, he moved to London to serve as secretary to Sir William Temple. With Temple's help, Swift obtained appointments with the Church of England in both England and Ireland. In 1713 he became the dean of Saint Patrick's Cathedral in Dublin, where he remained for the rest of his life; when historians of the Protestant Ascendancy refer to "the dean," they are talking about Swift.

SATIRE AT ITS FINEST

Jonathan Swift's *Gulliver's Travels* can be appreciated at many levels; it is at the same time an amusing adventure story and a scathing critique of humanity's laws. The book was an extraordinary success in its own day, and its popularity has continued into modern times.

In his early career, Swift used his talents for satire and allegory in addressing political causes. His work skillfully articulated the positions of the Tory Party while skewering his enemies. As his career progressed, he increasingly identified with Ireland. His "Drapier's Letters" (1724), which helped block an English coinage scheme that would have debased the Irish currency, made him a hero in Dublin. "A Modest Proposal" (1729) satirically argued that Irish families could address poverty and overpopulation by selling their children as food. It was a bitterly ironic attack against Whig policies of ignoring Irish social problems.

Swift's greatest work was not so much an attack on a political enemy as a criticism of human irrationality. *Gulliver's Travels* (1726) is a satire in the form of a fantastic travel journal. Lemuel Gulliver, a ship's physician, voyages to four exotic lands: Lilliput, where no one is more than 6 inches tall; Brobdingnag, a land of giants; Laputa, an empire run by wise men; and Houyhnhnmland, where the Houyhnhnms and the Yahoos live.

WHAT FAMOUS AUTHOR DID PREJUDICE LEAVE PENNILESS?

Oscar Wilde produced some of the late nineteenth century's most brilliant plays. The tragedy of his career is that prejudice snuffed out his incandescent wit in its prime.

Oscar Wilde was born into a home where his creativity could reign free: his father was a famously eccentric surgeon, and his mother, "Speranza" Wilde, was a well-known socialite and writer of nationalist poetry. With his privileged background, Wilde was able to study at Oxford, where he became a disciple of Walter Pater and led the aesthetic movement, in which he advocated the idea of "art for art's sake." He was famous for his long hair, his eccentric dress, and his habit of carrying flowers everywhere. His idiosyncrasies were satirized in Gilbert and Sullivan's *Patience* (1881).

Wilde married Constance Lloyd in 1884 and the couple settled in London. He wrote poems and children's books for a few years, and then in 1891 he emerged as a literary star with *The Picture of Dorian Gray*. The novel is about the moral degeneration of a man who is kept young by a mystical painting that reflects his true age and corruption. Wilde followed this novel with a string of brilliantly witty plays, including *Lady Windermere's Fan* (1892), *Salomé* (1893), *An Ideal Husband* (1895), and *The Importance of Being Earnest* (1895). For a while, he was the toast of London.

Unfortunately, tragedy brought him down. Wilde was a homosexual, and he had carried on an affair with Lord Alfred Douglas for some time. Douglas's father, the marquis of Queensberry, accused Wilde of committing sodomy, a crime in Victorian England. Wilde sued the marquis for libel, but after a sensational trial Wilde was convicted and sentenced to two years of hard labor. His incarceration left him physically, financially, and spiritually ruined. He fled to Paris, where he died, broken and penniless, in 1900.

WHAT POET WON THE NOBEL PRIZE IN LITERATURE IN 1923?

William Butler Yeats is widely considered to be one of the greatest poets of the twentieth century. He was born in Dublin in 1865 to an Anglo-Irish landowning family. His father, John Butler Yeats, was a well-known painter. Yeats spent much of his childhood in County Sligo, in West Ireland. He pursued painting as a young man, but he soon decided that his true passion was poetry.

The first inspirations for Yeats's poetry were the landscape, language, and mythology of Sligo. The folktales he heard from the local people led him to develop a fascination with Celtic stories and mysticism that influenced his work throughout his life. In the 1880s he became one of the leading voices promoting the study of Irish language and folklore. His poems, such as "The Wanderings of Oisin" (1889) and "The Lake Isle of Innisfree" (1893), communicated his love of Celtic myth to a wider audience.

Although he shunned violence, Yeats was passionately committed to the idea of an independent Irish state. The heroine of his play *Cathleen ni Houlihan* (1902) became a symbol of the Nationalist movement. One of his best-known poems, "Easter 1916," expressed his powerful conflicting emotions on the hope and violence embodied in the 1916 Easter Rebellion.

Yeats was a prolific and versatile writer throughout his career. His work in drama, folklore, and essays would each independently have made him a luminary of Irish literature. His true genius, however, came out in his poetry. In 1923, the year the Irish Free State was declared, Yeats won the Nobel Prize in literature "for his always inspired poetry, which in a highly artistic form gives expression to the spirit of a whole nation."

WHAT REVOLUTIONARY NOVELIST EXILED HIMSELF FROM IRELAND?

James Joyce revolutionized the novel, the short story, and modern literature as we know it. He was born in Dublin, the first of ten children in a Catholic family. His father was a civil servant whose poor financial judgment left the family impoverished for much of Joyce's youth. Joyce attended Dublin's fine Jesuit schools, which gave him a firm grounding in theology and classical languages—subjects that repeatedly appeared in his later work. The story of his early life and his intellectual rebellion against Catholicism and Irish Nationalism are told in the largely autobiographical novel *A Portrait of the Artist as a Young Man* (1916), originally published in 1904 as *Stephen Hero*.

In 1902, at the age of twenty, Joyce left Dublin to spend the rest of his life in Paris, Trieste, Rome, and Zurich, with only occasional visits back home. Despite this self-imposed exile, Dublin was the setting for most of his writings. *The Dubliners* (1914) is a collection of short stories describing the paralyzing social mores of middle-class Catholic life. Its style is more accessible than most of Joyce's work. "The Dead," the final story in the collection, is frequently listed as one of the finest short stories ever written.

Joyce spent seven years working on *Ulysses* (1922); once he finished writing it, he had a difficult time finding someone to publish it. Once it was published, Ireland and the United States immediately banned it as obscene, and most people who located copies found the writing nearly incomprehensible. Despite these obstacles, *Ulysses* has come to be generally recognized as the most influential English novel of the twentieth century.

WHICH IRISH WRITER WROTE PRIMARILY IN FRENCH?

Samuel Beckett was born in Dublin to a middle-class Protestant family. After an education at Trinity College, he moved to Paris, where he befriended James Joyce and became involved in the Parisian literary scene. Beckett experimented with various styles during this period, producing poems, novels, and short stories that were popular in French critical circles. During World War II, Beckett stayed in France and was active in the Resistance.

In the postwar years, Beckett began to find true success by evolving his own style and writing primarily in French (he usually translated the English versions himself). He wrote a critically acclaimed trilogy of novels: *Molloy, Malone Dies*, and *The Unnameable*. His greatest successes were his plays, particularly *Waiting for Godot* and *Endgame*. In 1969 Beckett received the Nobel Prize in literature "for his writing, which—in new forms for the novel and drama—in the destitution of modern man acquires its elevation" (in other words, for inventing absurdist drama). He produced a number of plays in the 1970s and 1980s, which were widely read but less original than his earlier works. He died in Paris in 1989.

WHICH IRISH POET IS FAMOUS FOR TRANSLATING *BEOWULF*?

The American poet Robert Lowell said that Seamus Heaney is the greatest Irish poet since Yeats: Oddly, he was born in the year of Yeats's death. Heaney was the oldest of nine children in a Catholic farming family in County Derry, Northern Ireland. At St. Columb's College in Derry and Queens University in Belfast, Heaney received a grounding in Latin, Irish, and Anglo-Saxon that has enriched the language of his poetry. The themes of his poems arose from the tensions of the land in which he lived: Ulster's industrial present versus its rural past; English roots versus Gaelic; and the rising conflict between Northern Ireland's Catholics and Protestants.

Heaney has produced a number of vibrant poetry collections: *Death of a Naturalist* (1966), *North* (1975), *Station Island* (1984), and *Seeing Things* (1991). In addition, he has written plays, essays, and a best-selling translation of the Anglo-Saxon epic *Beowulf* (1999). Heaney received the 1995 Nobel Prize in literature "for works of lyrical beauty and ethical depth, which exalt everyday miracles and the living past."

WHICH IRISH NOVELIST INVENTED THE WORLD'S MOST FAMOUS VAMPIRE?

Abraham "Bram" Stoker was born to a middle-class family near Dublin. After a successful stint at Trinity College, he entered the civil service in Dublin. His life took a turn for the dramatic, however, when some amateur theater criticism he had written came to the attention of Sir Henry Irving, one of the pre-eminent actors in England at that time. The two met and immediately became friends. Soon afterward, Stoker quit the civil service and moved to London to serve as Irving's full-time manager.

THE COUNT OF THE CATACOMBS

St. Michan's Church in Dublin is charming on the surface, but underneath it lie crypts of ancient, creepy horror. Originally built during Viking times, the limestone catacombs boast an unusual combination of cool, dry air that has somehow preserved dozens of corpses within. It is thought that St. Michan's mummies inspired Bram Stoker's story of a man who would not die—Count Dracula.

While working in the London theater scene, Stoker wrote a number of eerie, gothic stories. The most famous of these was *Dracula* (1897), which introduced the world's most famous vampire. The story of good versus evil became an international bestseller that has remained popular into the present day. It's been said that Count Dracula has appeared in more movies than any other fictional character. Stoker's other popular works include *The Jewel of Seven Stars* (1904) and *The Lair of the White Worm* (1911).

PART 15

Geography and Climate

Ireland's physical environment has always had a tremendous impact on the lives of its people. Its land, waters, and wildlife have determined what people eat and how they live. Its geographic location has played a large part in its political history, protecting it from some European armies and exposing it to others. In modern times, Ireland's great natural beauty has helped build a booming tourist industry. What do you know about Ireland's wet climate and rugged landscape?

WHERE IS THE SUNNIEST PART OF THE EMERALD ISLE?

The southeastern corner of Ireland is separated from the rest of the island by the Wicklow Mountains, which form a natural barrier from western attackers. The people here have historically had more to do with England and Europe than have people in the rest of Ireland. The Vikings settled here, especially in Waterford, Wexford, Wicklow, and Arklow. The southeast is known to have more sunny days than the rest of the island, and the local geography and sea currents have produced a string of calm, sandy beaches along the coast. These beaches attract tourists from Ireland and all over Europe.

WHAT'S SO SPECIAL ABOUT THE KERRY PENINSULA?

The southwest of Ireland is one of the most beautiful parts of the island. The Kerry Peninsula juts out into the Atlantic, a landscape of rugged cliffs descending into crashing waves. The Gulf Stream warms the coast, making the area fertile to both plants and animals. Seabirds love the islands off the coast; the Skellig Islands are home to many gannets, and the aptly named Puffin Island is home to thousands of puffins. Cork has long been the port from which people come and go to the European continent, and Kerry has been the traditional point of departure for the Americas. The Dingle and Iveragh peninsulas are very isolated from the rest of Ireland; for this reason the Irish language has survived there.

WHAT PART OF IRELAND HELPED PRESERVE THE COUNTRY'S CULTURE?

The west of Ireland, traditionally called Connacht, includes the Counties Mayo, Galway, Leitrim, Sligo, and Roscommon. The region is beautiful but quite rocky. The cliffs, although dramatic, don't offer many good places to launch or land boats. That's why people in the west have congregated around Galway Bay and the Shannon Estuary, which offer relatively safer waters. Though it's no farmer's paradise, even rocky Connacht can support quite a few people; before the Great Famine of the 1840s, Ireland's rocky west was feeding a good portion of Ireland's 8 million people with potatoes grown on hillsides.

The Connemara Mountains and the Aran Islands are stunningly beautiful and full of history; early Christians sought out these remote areas as safe havens. The Irish fled (or were banished) to these areas when the English took over, and the remoteness helped them preserve their culture and language. Connacht continues to be home to a number of Irish speakers. County Sligo was the favorite landscape of William Butler Yeats, who celebrated the region in his poems.

WHERE'S THE BEST PLACE TO CATCH IRISH LOBSTER?

Up in the northwest corner is County Donegal, a remote area of mountains and beaches. The coastline is full of jagged cliffs, home to seabirds that enjoy fishing in the ocean there. Humans also fish; lobster is one of the most important catches in the area. However, Donegal's most famous product is its tweed cloth, traditionally dyed brown with a fungus scraped off local rocks.

SHOULD YOU PACK A RAINCOAT?

Even though Ireland lies far to the north, its climate is quite mild. The Gulf Stream current in the Atlantic moderates the weather, preventing extremes of either heat or cold. It seldom freezes in winter and snows very little. Summer temperatures are pleasantly warm but very rarely hot. Within this moderate range, though, temperatures can be unpredictable; sometimes it is terribly cold in July or quite warm in January.

LET IN THE LIGHT!

People are often surprised at how far north Ireland is—it's on the same latitude as Newfoundland. In the summer, daylight can last for eighteen hours; in the winter, nights are long and days are very short.

What is predictable is rain. Ireland gets a lot of rain. Some regions, such as County Kerry in the southwest, enjoy up to 270 rainy days a year. The prevailing winds come from the southwest, picking up rain clouds in the Atlantic and then dumping them on the island. All this rain makes Ireland a paradise for green growing things—hence its nickname, the Emerald Isle.

WHAT ARE IRELAND'S LARGEST LAKE AND LONGEST RIVER?

Ireland is full of picturesque lakes, gouged out by glaciers during the last Ice Age. The lakes near Killarney have stunned visitors for years. Lough Neagh in Northern Ireland is Ireland's largest lake.

Ireland is also full of rivers, which have allowed people to penetrate the island's interior either to settle it or to attack it. The Shannon is the longest river; it runs from County Cavan to the Shannon Estuary between Counties Clare and Limerick, traveling more than 230 miles across the middle of the island.

HOW DID DEFORESTATION AFFECT IRELAND?

In prehistoric times, Ireland was covered with forests. Most of these trees were oaks, mixed with birch and pine on the hills and with elm, alder, ash, and hawthorn in the lower areas. Other plants grew under the trees. The forest was home to a large variety of animal species.

Farmers started cutting down trees about 6,000 years ago, but deforestation didn't become rampant until the 1500s. At that time the English occupiers cut down most of Ireland's oak to use in shipbuilding and barrel making. By the eighteenth century, Ireland had very little forest left and had to import most of its wood. In the twentieth century, Irish people began planting tree farms, and now about 5 percent of the country is covered with trees again. Most of that is commercially grown pine, but some people are planting oaks and other native trees again.

The forests have been replaced with natural bogs and man-made agricultural fields. Ireland has long been a great place to farm; even the most marginal land on hillsides can support bumper crops of potatoes, though it's not good for much else. The richest soil is in central and eastern Ireland, east of the Shannon River. The west is rockier and not especially good for agriculture; that's why Oliver Cromwell banished rebellious Irish out there, keeping the better land for his own supporters.

WHERE DOES PEAT COME FROM?

The bogs are lush wetlands where plants grow thickly on top of shallow water (the ground is mushy, but you can walk on it). When the plants died, there wasn't enough oxygen in the water for them to rot quickly, so over the years a dense layer of plant matter accumulated to form peat. These bogs can be 20 to 40 feet thick.

For centuries the Irish people have used peat from the bogs to fuel their fires. They cut chunks of peat every spring and set them out to dry in the sun; then they burned the dried peat, also called sod or turf, in their fireplaces. Few families still burn peat these days, but a substantial portion of Ireland's electricity comes from peat-burning power plants.

PETRIFIED BUTTER

Bogs are so oxygen-poor that things buried in them often don't rot. Archaeologists have found tools, weapons, jewelry, and even well-preserved human bodies in the bogs. The real treat, though, is bog butter; people buried huge clumps of butter in the cool peat to keep them fresh, but forgot to dig them up. Today, museums across the midlands proudly display these ancient chunks of petrified dairy fat. Sounds delicious!

Bogs support their own unique ecosystems, with spectacular flowers and plants that have evolved to thrive in the unusual environment, including carnivorous plants that eat insects. The bogs are also an important habitat for birds.

Bogs used to cover one-seventh of Ireland's landscape, but they have been depleted over the years. In the twentieth century, the Irish Peat Board excavated thousands of acres of bog to sell to power companies and other businesses that used the peat—they turned it into briquettes for burning and sold it to garden companies as compost. Some people fear that the bogs could disappear completely in the near future. Now the Irish Wildlife Service and the Peat Board are working together to preserve Ireland's remaining bogs, which they consider a national treasure.

WHAT'S THE BURREN?

The Burren in County Clare is barren and bleak. It's a startling place, a giant field of limestone slabs that look like a slightly greener version of the moon's surface. The slabs are dotted with big limestone boulders. Below ground are caves hollowed out by millions of years of running water; some people make a hobby out of mapping this cave system.

Ireland has lots of limestone under its rich soil and greenery, but the Burren is the only place where most of it is exposed, because glaciers from the last Ice Age scraped away the topsoil about 15,000 years ago. The surface of the limestone is quite dry; all water that falls on it quickly drips down to the network of underground streams. The Burren has a few lakes, but they are prone to disappearing suddenly when the water table drops.

Though it looks bleak, the Burren supports an astonishing array of plant life. Beautiful flowering plants, such as foxgloves, rock roses, and a number of orchids, thrive on the limestone. Grass grows there, too, in the hollows of the rocks; the limestone stores heat, which allows the grass to grow year-round. A number of wild goats live off this grass. Sometimes farmers even move their cattle to the Burren to graze.

People have lived in the area of the Burren for millennia, long before the Celts arrived. Some seventy ancient tombs are there, including the Poulnabrone dolmen, constructed about 4,500 years ago, and the Gleninsheen wedge tomb, where a wonderful gold collar dating from about 700 B.C.E. was found.

DID GIANTS REALLY BUILD THE GIANT'S CAUSEWAY?

The Giant's Causeway, on the coast of northern County Antrim, is one of the more stupendous sights in the world. It is a collection of bizarre rock formations set between the sea and the towering cliffs. Most of them are hexagonal columns that stand straight up from the ground. The flat tops of the columns look like stepping stones, and visitors can actually walk on them. Some of the odder formations have colorful names such as Giant's Eyes (circular bubbles of basalt rock) and the Giant's Organ (columns of rock that look like the pipes of an organ). Others include the King and His Nobles, the Chimney Tops, the Honeycomb, the Giant's Loom, and the Wishing Chair.

The name "Giant's Causeway" comes from a legend about Finn MacCool, who supposedly built it. (Finn was sometimes spoken of as a giant.) In this story, he was spectacularly huge, and he had fallen in love with Una, a large and luscious lady on Staffa Island, off the Scottish coast (which is across from this part of Ireland and happens to have the same bizarre, honeycomb-shaped rock formations as the Giant's Causeway). Finn built the causeway as a bridge between the two islands so he could take Una home with him. Everything was going swimmingly until Benandonner, an even more spectacularly large Scottish giant, decided to come after them and take Una back to be his girlfriend.

Finn was tough, but when he saw Benandonner's immense bulk, he realized the Scot was just too big to fight. Fortunately, Finn was also clever—with Una's help, he disguised himself as an immense Irish infant. When Benandonner saw how big Irish babies were, he got scared of facing a full-grown one, and he ran back to Scotland, destroying the causeway in the process. That's why all we have left today are the remnants on the North Antrim coast and on Staffa Island.

Geologists, however, believe that volcanic eruptions and the rapid cooling of tholeiitic basalt lava 60 million years ago resulted in the unusual polygonal shapes. Retreating glaciers exposed the basalt columns 15,000 years ago, and the Giant's Causeway was born.

WHY IS BIRD WATCHING SO POPULAR IN IRELAND?

Bird watchers love western Ireland because its cliffs and islands are a favorite breeding location for seabirds. Puffins, cormorants, herons, and other birds lay their eggs there; their colonies cover the cliff sides in the springtime. Ireland is also a stopover on the migration routes of many Arctic and African birds. One of these African visitors is the corncrake, which comes to Ireland to breed in April. It is terribly endangered because its nesting areas have all become farmland, but people are now trying to preserve it.

WHY IS IRELAND FAMOUS FOR ITS HORSES?

Horses have lived in Ireland for about 4,000 years, and they seem to find the environment quite congenial. Some people claim the limestone underneath Irish soil makes the grass there especially good for growing strong bones in horses. Irish racehorses and show horses are known for their strength and beauty. In the eighteenth and nineteenth centuries, the monarchs of Europe sought their horses in Ireland; Napoleon supposedly got his horse Marengo from the Emerald Isle. The Irish people take advantage of their terrain to create unique horse races, galloping their steeds on the beach or through the rough countryside.

PUT OUT TO PASTURE

The Irish National Stud in Kildare is the nation's pre-eminent site for horse breeding. The accompanying museum explains the rich heritage of Irish horse racing. Exceptionally beautiful horses can be seen here, and the surrounding green hills make fantastic horse pasture.

Smaller but sturdier ponies also thrive in Ireland. Connemara ponies live in Connemara in the west, where they grow small but rugged, eating the local sea grass. The rare Kerry Bog pony lives in County Kerry. These ponies probably developed from ponies brought over from Spain in the 1600s. Kerry Bog ponies are tough and strong, good at hauling loads of turf or seaweed. Large herds of them used to live in Kerry, but their numbers dwindled in the nineteenth century. Enthusiasts are now breeding them again.

WHY IS IRELAND INTERESTED IN PRESERVING ITS NATURAL ENVIRONMENT?

Like many developed countries, Ireland has recently become interested in preserving its natural environment and saving endangered species. A governmental organization called Dúchas monitors national parks and gardens. The Irish Wildlife Trust oversees wilderness areas. The National Trust, called An Taisce in Ireland, preserves important natural sites and historical structures. These organizations are all working to designate and protect areas of natural and cultural significance, and to make them accessible to visitors.

Ireland also boasts five national parks:

- ♣ The Burren
- ♣ Connemara
- ♣ Glenveagh
- ♣ Killarney
- ♣ Wicklow Mountains

In addition, there are several forest parks, an area of blanket bog in County Mayo, and a number of National Nature Reserves.

The Irish interest in protecting the beauty of their natural landscape will benefit all who are interested in Ireland. Ireland's varied and picturesque terrain makes it one of the most charming countries in the world to visit. The appeal of the landscape, however, is more than just visual. Ireland's geography—its location, climate, and natural resources—has played a crucial role in the political and cultural development of the Irish people. To understand Irish history and heritage, it's important to appreciate the land itself.

AFTERWORD

The face of Ireland is changing. The charming but patron-
izing images of the past—the simple farmer, the friendly
drunk—have given way to the real faces of Seamus Heaney,
U2's Bono, and Mary Robinson, the first female president.
In the midst of all this change, however, Ireland has not
forgotten where it came from. The Irish people look to their
past for education and inspiration. It isn't difficult, because
the past is all around them: Stone Age tombs exist alongside
monastic round towers; modern-day bards perform Celtic
tunes in Anglo-Irish mansions. We hope you now know
more about the beauty, conflict, and culture of this rugged
land and will continue to watch as the many elements of Ireland's rich heritage blend with its present to make Ireland a
beautiful and fascinating place.

APPENDIX
A Primer of the Irish Language

If you're interested in learning more about the Irish language or want to try to speak it on your own, you'll find here a pronunciation guide and some common words and phrases to help you speak like you're from the Emerald Isle. After all, it might be easier to gain the gift of gab if you can say a few words in Ireland's original tongue!

IRISH PRONUNCIATION

Irish has three main dialects, Connacht, Munster, and Ulster; each of these has its own pronunciation quirks. Schools teach a standardized form of Irish that combines features of these three dialects.

VOWELS

Irish marks long vowels with an accent; short vowels have no accent. Here are the main vowel sounds:

- *a* as in "bat"
- *á* as "aw"
- *e* as in "pet"
- *é* as in "gray"
- *i* as in "hit"

- *í* as in "fee"
- *o* as in "son"
- *ó* as in "glow"
- *u* as in "took"
- *ú* as in "rule"

DIPHTHONGS AND TRIPHTHONGS

Diphthongs are two vowels stuck together, and triphthongs are three vowels put together. You use them all the time in English without even thinking about it. Here are some common Irish diphthongs and triphthongs:

- *ia* as "ee-a"
- *ai* and *ea* as "ah"
- *ua* as "oo-a"
- *ei* as "eh"
- *eu* as "ai," as in "air"
- *oi* as "uh-ee"
- *ae* as in "cat"
- *io* and *ui* as "ih," as in "ill"
- *ao* as "oo"

- *eo* as "uh"
- *éo* as "yo"
- *aí* as "ee"
- *iu* as "yew"
- *aoi* as "ee"
- *ái* as "awee" or "oy"
- *eoi* as "oh-ih"
- *éi* as "ayee"
- *eái* as "ah-ih"

- *ói* as "oh-ee"
- *iai* as "ee-ah-ee"
- *úi* as "oo-ee"
- *uai* as "oo-ih"

- *eá* as "ah"
- *iui* as "ew-ih"
- *ío* as "ee"

CONSONANTS

Irish has many clusters of consonants that have their own idiosyncratic pronunciations:

- *bh* as "v"
- *bhf* as "w"
- *c* as "k"
- *ch* as a guttural sound, like the "ch" in "Loch Ness"
- *d* as "d" when followed by a broad vowel, and as "j" when followed by a slender vowel
- *dh* as "g" when followed by a broad vowel, as "y" when followed by a slender vowel

- *mh* as "w"
- *s* as "s" before a broad vowel, as "sh" before a slender vowel or at the end of the word
- *t* as "t" before a broad vowel, as "ch" before a slender vowel
- *th* as the "h" in "house"; at the end of a word, either silent or pronounced as the "t" in "hat"

BASIC WORDS AND PHRASES

Here are a few common greetings and pleasantries:

- Please: *Le do thoil* (le do hall)
- Thank you: *Go raibh maith agat* (go rev mut agut)
- You're welcome: *Tá fáilte romhat* (taw foil-cha row-ath) or just *fáilte*
- Hello (to one person): *Dia duit* (dee-a gwit)

- Hello (to several people): *Dia daoibh* (dee-a gweev)
- Hello (in response to greeting): *Dia's Muire duit* (dee-as mwir-a gwit)
- Goodbye (to a person leaving): *Slán leat* (slawn lath)
- Goodbye (to a person staying behind): *Slán agat* (slawn agut)
- Good night: *Oíche mhaith* (ee-ha ho)
- Cheers (literally "health"): *Sláinte* (slan-chuh)

INDEX

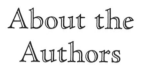

About the Authors

Ryan Hackney received his BA and MA in the history of science from Harvard University. He lives in Houston, TX.

Amy Hackney Blackwell graduated from Duke University with degrees in history and medieval and renaissance studies. She received her MA in early modern European history from Vanderbilt University. She lives in Greenville, SC.